# ADDICTED

# DOWNLOAD THE AUDIOBOOK FREE!

### READ THIS FIRST

To say thank you for purchasing my book,
I would like to give you the Audiobook version
100% Free.

I know you are more likely to finish this book
if you have the audiobook, too.

I even narrated the book so it will feel more like
I'm personally sharing my story with you.

Now you won't have to pay $10 - $20 for the audiobook.

### ADDICTED-BOOK.COM/AUDIO

# ADDICTED

Recovering from Marijuana Addiction

Kathy D.

Copyright © by Kathy D. 2022
All rights reserved

ISBN: 979-8-88759-284-8 12.95 (paperback)
ISBN: 979-8-88759-285-5 7.95 (ebook)

*For every single person who picks up marijuana and one day discovers they can't put it down and don't know what to do next.*

# Contents

Introduction ................................................................. ix

**Part 1: From Birth to Rebirth** ................................................ 1

    Chapter 1:    Innocent Beginnings ................................. 3

    Chapter 2:    Domestic Warzone .................................... 11

    Chapter 3:    Coming of Age ......................................... 21

    Chapter 4:    From Magic to Madness ......................... 27

    Chapter 5:    A Progressive Disease .............................. 33

    Chapter 6:    Am I A Marijuana Addict? ..................... 41

    Chapter 7:    An Experiment ......................................... 53

    Chapter 8:    We Don't Want You Here ....................... 57

    Chapter 9:    From Sobriety to Recovery ..................... 63

**Part 2: After I Quit Smoking Weed** .......................................... 71

    Chapter 10:    Detoxification ........................................ 75

    Chapter 11:    Who Am I Recovering For? .................. 81

    Chapter 12:    Finding A Tribe ..................................... 85

    Chapter 13:    Finding A Guide ................................... 95

    Chapter 14:    Changing Our Surroundings ............... 103

    Chapter 15:    The Steps to Restoration ..................... 107

    Chapter 16:    From Selfish and Self-Seeking to Selfless Service ................................................... 113

**Part 3: Recovery Is Simple, but It's Not Easy ............... 119**
    Chapter 17:    Avoid Romancing the Stone ..................121
    Chapter 18:    Progress Not Perfection ........................127
    Chapter 19:    One Day At A Time ............................137
    Chapter 20:    The Gifts of Addiction Recovery ..........143

Recovery Resources ......................................................147

Acknowledgments ........................................................155

Author Bio ...................................................................157

# INTRODUCTION

Hi. I'm guessing that if you picked up this book, maybe you aren't doing well, or you use marijuana and you're wondering if you might be an addict. Or maybe you seek understanding because you know someone who uses marijuana.

I started smoking marijuana regularly when I was eighteen. Many people start much earlier, at eleven or twelve.

I've witnessed hundreds of people pass through the "rooms of recovery," support meetings for those who chose a life of sobriety. Some people come in, answering an ultimatum from a parent, spouse, or employer, who caught them smoking weed. Other people appear with a court card, requiring proof of attendance, and are not usually seen again after the card is full. A few come looking for a solution to their out-of-control marijuana use. Many of those people found a marijuana recovery program by accident, often stating that they had no idea there was one. In the meetings, some shared that they didn't think marijuana was addictive. In fact, sometimes, using becomes addictive for some but not for others.

Me? I am a marijuana addict. Plain and simple. My story starts with alcohol. I am a periodic alcoholic; I did not drink all day every day, but after the first drink of the day, I didn't stop until I threw up or passed out. I also had a few brief, intense bouts with cocaine, crack, and methamphetamine. The only constant, however, was marijuana. Pot was reliable for a long time. It didn't make me feel sick or jittery, and it mellowed me out when I got too drunk or was going too fast. I smoked cannabis long after it was enjoyable or fun for me. I thought I could quit until I tried. I've been practicing a program of addiction recovery for over eighteen years. Make that *eighteen years* since 2003. And I've learned a few things about the disease of addiction, enough that today—sober and recovering—I have many insights and experiences to pass on to you, regardless of the substance you chose.

Through reading a variety of literature about drug abuse, I discovered that the problem with addiction to any substance is that the substance—alcohol, marijuana, heroin, speed, food, sex, video games, streaming movies, etcetera—is not the problem. Don't get me wrong; it certainly becomes a problem. It's just that the addiction is a *symptom*—a visible indicator—of deeper issues. In my case, it never crossed my mind that I had any issues that needed addressing. If I had, I was certainly not equipped to handle or deal with them in a healthy manner. Pot, for me, was the solution to avoiding those buried issues for as long as I could. And it worked until it didn't.

When my solution—marijuana—stopped working, I needed a new solution and had no idea where to look.

So, I kept on smoking *until I was arrested*. During the court process, I was introduced to a recovery program for marijuana addicts, a program that is still surprising people daily by its very existence.

What qualifies me to share my journey with you? I think it starts with getting clean and sober, then *staying* clean and sober since 2003, through many situations and circumstances that once sent me running to my bedroom, opening the top drawer of my nightstand, and pulling out my weed in the first place.

## Introduction

This book is the abbreviated story of how I went from entrenched addiction to finding recovery while often kicking and screaming and the many ways in which my life got better. I'll share stories about my life before and just after I began using marijuana. Stories that illustrate what eventually happened, encouraging me to change my behavior and how I did that with the help of strangers who were like me. I don't quote stats, for the most part, or include charts about how many addicts there are or how many get clean and sober following the program I follow.

Instead, I offer experience, strength, and hope with the aspiration that you will read it and find something here that will help you take the next step if you decide marijuana is a problem in your life.

I realize I cannot possibly relay all the experiences I've had or all the things I've learned over the past twenty years. I'll do my best to give you the most memorable, moving moments, both during active addiction and in my recovery.

There are many benefits when working a program of recovery. One benefit was the return of my dignity. In truth, I was marijuana's bitch, and today that is not okay with me. I would have done anything for that feeling of invincibility and fearlessness, and I did. After I chose to try sobriety, I began to value myself more than I valued the induced relaxation and emotional detachment I had been a slave to. That feeling was fleeting, and recovery is proving to be consistent and lasting, just so long as I keep doing the deal.

Financially, I stopped spending hundreds of dollars on marijuana and discovered I had much more money than I realized. Physically, I have renewed power loads of energy. I lost that raspy smoker's cough and the phlegm that came with it. I slept better, and I cried less. I stopped raging when I didn't get my way, and I found some peace.

Once, years into my recovery life, I had the urge to smoke again. *Why,* I asked myself, *would you ever want to jeopardize all you've gained by taking just* one *more taste of that plant?*

I cannot provide statistical proof regarding the effectiveness of the tips I share in this book. I *can* tell you confidently they worked for me and are working for hundreds of people I've met over the years—in rehabilitation clinics, in recovery meetings, across the United States at various recovery conferences and conventions, and, by God's grace, in total strangers—former active addicts who now live useful, fulfilling lives in sobriety.

I cannot guarantee that you will never use marijuana again. I will tell you that you *never have to* if you don't want to, and you get to decide.

I can promise you that everything I share with you is true for me. I have stayed clean and sober, and my life has gone through monumental shifts. It's different now—mostly better—often challenging. Sometimes *very* challenging. I have experienced many triumphs, and in all these eighteen years of sobriety, not once have I found a convincing enough reason to throw away all the blessings and gifts for a little more time with weed. If it ever calls, the call goes unanswered.

I also promise you this: if you do what you've always done, you'll get what you've always gotten. If you are tired of getting what you've always gotten and want to try something unfamiliar, uncomfortable, and different—with the promise of getting something new, wonderful, and sometimes painful for a brief period—this book is for you. If you implement the tools I share in it—learned through study, research, trial and error, and time—you can get clean and sober and stay clean and sober. It's all on you, though. No one can do this for you; you should only do it for yourself. You just don't have to do it alone.

# Introduction

Today is the first day of the rest of your life, and if you are anything like me, you've already spent too many days dreaming big dreams and sitting around waiting for them to materialize magically. There is no time like the present to get off your "but" and do something new before the *yets* start happening, like, "I haven't been arrested *yet*, evicted *yet*, fired *yet*, gone bankrupt *yet*, fucked up my relationship or my kids *yet*." The list goes on and on.

That you picked up this book indicates at least a curiosity about the topic and an interest in learning more about cannabis addiction and recovery. If you have the time, my suggestion to you is that you take twenty minutes a day to read this book, try some of the actions I've outlined, and see if your day-to-day outlook on life improves. If you are already desperate and the *yets* are happening now, jump to Part Two immediately and review the detox chapter and six basic life changes I've outlined that made all the difference in early recovery.

Today is the first day of the rest of your life. How you proceed from here is up to you. Know this: you don't have to do it alone.

## PART ONE

# From Birth to Rebirth

*I*t was never my ambition to become a marijuana addict. If you'd suggested to me that it was even a thing, I'd have disagreed. As a kid, life seemed ideal. I had two parents, and I felt happy. I had some friends, and I had toys. I was a good student. When I was young, I had a picture-perfect life.

Then life threw some curveballs. My parents surprised my brother and me with a divorce. Later, my dad surprised us with a mentally unstable woman who became our stepmother. Remember *Cinderella*? Ursula nailed it and then some.

Trust was shattered by betrayal. We learned to pretend that everything happening around us was normal; that everyone experienced it. As I got older, I realized that not everyone lived in a household like ours.

In my story, pretending and lying became the curriculum for an education in denial. If I could pretend that my father and his wife, who constantly and violently fought with each other, also loved each other, then I could pretend all kinds of things. When I told the truth and was called a liar repeatedly, I learned to lie—to give them what they were looking for so they would go away.

By age eleven, I was withdrawing into myself, adopting the philosophy of every man for himself and every woman for herself. *I'd love to help you, but I'm barely treading water.* I excelled where it mattered. I did my chores as if I had a PhD in cleaning. I was an overachieving student and child. I did everything better than required to keep any negative focus off of me. It wasn't foolproof. Self-preservation is a powerful motivator, though.

Until my sophomore year of high school, I was holding my own. Then the wheels of my life got a little wobbly. And following my dad's second divorce, I took a detour through the county's juvenile detention program. But in a couple of years, I was back on the overachieving track, honing my people-pleasing skills and improving my pretending and lying, mostly for my own benefit.

Carrying those learned early childhood skills into adulthood, I added pot smoking partier to the resume. I didn't become an addict overnight, but I was willing to put in the work.

At the end of a couple of decades of using marijuana and alcohol to maintain the illusion that life was just fine, things began to unravel in a way that I had to really notice. I got tired of trying to keep up the charade. I heard a guy say this recently, "I was at the party, and the music was pumping, and I just wanted the music to stop."

The end was like a plane landed by an amateur. In my attempts to put the plane on the ground, I hit the runway several times, and when I finally landed, I hit the brakes a little too hard, screeching to an abrupt halt.

It's taken me almost nineteen years to repair the damage that occurred before I ever picked up a joint and after I committed to the fairytale that I could have it all. I told myself I could do it better than the last guy.

In the next several chapters, I will share, where relevant, what it was like for me growing up before I picked up an illegal substance, and how I fell into the grips of drug addiction.

If you are wondering where you fit in, I have some answers. I promise that if you are an addict, you'll recognize yourself in these pages, and you'll realize hope is waiting.

# CHAPTER ONE

## Innocent Beginnings

Looking back over my life, I recognize key moments that I believe shaped my response to life—well before I started drinking or using marijuana regularly—though I didn't know it at the time. Now I see those moments as contributing factors reinforcing my desire to avoid pain and consequences.

For starters, my mother gave birth to me in a hospital for unwed mothers.

My parents met on a blind date, and following a brief interlude of dating, I was conceived. My mother shared with me that my grandmother and great-grandmother drove her to Mexico early in her pregnancy for an illegal abortion. They angrily disapproved of my mother's situation. At the last minute, when she was about to be admitted, she refused treatment and ran blindly from the clinic through the dark alleys of Tijuana, adrenaline pumping.

Back in Los Angeles, she decided to place me in adoption and carried me full term, hidden away in a home for unwed mothers. When I was born, nuns took me from my mother's body and carried me away—not permitting my mother to even see me, adding a level of shame to her seemingly ruined life and robbing me of a bonding opportunity as well.

When a baby is born, the level of oxytocin—a chemical messenger that bonds mother to child—is very high; it helps soothe the baby and helps the infant identify its mother. Skin-to-skin contact is essential to this process. I did not bond properly with my mother—I didn't feel my mother's skin until I was thirty days old. How did I get to connect with my mother's skin after thirty days when I'd been signed away for adoption? I'm glad you asked.

Many years into my life, I discovered this story. After I was born, my father, a nineteen-year-old kid, showed up at my grandma's home with a change of heart. Despite originally taking his father's advice to run for the hills, in an act of bravery, my father asked my mother to give him a chance and marry him so they could raise me together. She grabbed that lifeline with both hands and pulled. But I believe the damage was already done.

In a nutshell, I was abandoned by my mother at birth. But then she, upon my father's arrival, changed her mind and reclaimed me. She married my dad, and they did their best. The letter from the adoption agency, releasing me back to my mother, still fills me with a swell of emotion when I read it. Only after my mother had died did I find the letter from the agency in her belongings.

My brother was born when I was two and a half years old. Although I couldn't articulate it at the time, I knew he was not an accident. He was accepted, loved, and coddled because of colic and breastfeeding issues. Not abandoned, he received my mother's primary attention. One could argue that he was a newborn and required that attention. They always had a bond that she and I did not.

What leads a person to addiction or alcoholism? I don't know.

I'll share a snippet from my memories that may support the idea that I was born that way, and somehow, the need to overindulge was in my genes. I was around four years old, and my parents were attending a party at the home of some friends. My brother and I, brought along to the party instead of left with a sitter, were tucked away in a guest bedroom. We lay awake in the dark room listening to the festivities in the other room. At some point, I crawled out of the warm twin bed where I'd been left and tiptoed from the dark bedroom down the hallway.

I vividly remember glancing through the open doorway that led to the living room where the adults were, toward the sounds of talking and laughing, ice cubes tinkling. Sounded like a fun time. I quickly, and quietly made my way to the bathroom. I was sitting on the toilet when an idea occurred to me. Did these people have that orange candy in their mirror cupboard like my mom did at home? I quickly climbed from the toilet seat cover onto the counter and over to the medicine cabinet. As I opened the cabinet, it squeaked just a bit. I froze.

No one came running, so I continued my quest. In the cabinet on a glass shelf sat a large plastic jar full of little orange tablets. Chewable baby aspirin. Prying open the lid, I poured three or four of those small tablets into my tiny, pudgy hand. Retwisting the top into place, I returned the bottle to its home on the shelf and carefully swung the cabinet's door shut. Then I climbed off the counter and snuck back down the long hall into the dark room. As I crawled onto the bed, I clasped the baby aspirin tightly in my sweaty little hand. I put one in my mouth and saw movement from the corner of my eye. My little brother—awake, standing in his playpen—spied me.

Holding his hand out, he moved his fingers in an opening and closing motion. I rolled off the bed and gave him a piece of my loot. If you've never had a chewable baby aspirin, you missed out. They're sweet, taste like oranges, and dissolve on your tongue. Honestly, I suppose I thought they were candy. What else could I have thought? I'd had to share with my brother and now had less tiny orange candy. I snuck back and forth from the bedroom to the bathroom multiple times before I was caught.

My two-year-old brother and I probably ate seventy-five of those baby aspirin each before my mother interrupted us. I remember how sick I felt before throwing up. I couldn't tell you if it was the aspirin or getting caught that caused my stomach to eject that delicious poison. Not lucky enough to throw up, my brother created some high tension and chaos. I vaguely remember he was taken to a hospital emergency room to have his stomach pumped. We lived through that adventure, and eventually, childproof bottles were created.

What possesses a four-year-old to consume half a bottle of baby aspirin? An addictive gene? The ignorance of the danger? Just some kind of crazy coincidence? After all, how could either of us have known the effect of that pill? Why would a harmful medicine taste so good?

I can trace a long line of alcoholics on both sides of my lineage. In life, however, I encountered plenty of reasons and opportunities to carry on the family legacy. Environment or a twisted gene? Other people arrived at my recovery meetings from ideal childhoods, excelling in school and receiving the love and support of their nonalcoholic, nonaddict parents. No matter. They still ended up sitting right next to me in the rooms of recovery. It takes all kinds.

The next few years were outwardly ideal. Then, starting in 1971, we began to move about once a year, each new house nicer than the last in a better neighborhood. Tension began to flare between my parents, but it was nothing my brother or I noticed. Except once.

It was another sunny summer day in southern California when my brother and I set out, riding our bikes to the corner market for candy. We wanted more than we could afford, so we took it. We *stole* wax lips and candy-covered chocolate bits from the store. Unknown to us, while we were riding home, the concerned and amused owner was phoning Mom. As we rode up the street toward our house, we saw our mother standing stiffly on the sidewalk, with hands on hips, the belt hanging to one side. My stomach became a ball of knots, and I felt sick inside. Nevertheless, I tried to play it cool. But she knew.

The tension I felt before being hit with that leather belt *increased* following my punishment. Mom didn't spank my brother. I felt anger. *He stole candy, too. Where was the justice?* Instead, she told my brother, who was maybe six, our father would deal with him when he got home. My anger dissolved, replaced by a feeling of fear for my brother. I'd much rather be spanked by my mom than my dad. I remember my mom shrinking a bit as she gave my brother that news. She seemed afraid then and somehow diminished. As if she'd lost a bet or drawn the short straw in a wager with my dad. That was the first time I could put my finger on a moment when I witnessed a strain in their relationship.

The trajectory of their lives and ours took an awful turn when I was nine.

One afternoon, the last day of third grade, I was hurrying home, excited about summer break, feeling so happy. Walking through the door, I smell cigarette smoke—Grandma! She'd come to take my brother and me away to her house. Felt like the best day ever!

Two weeks later, my dad is in Grandma's living room—alone—to pick us up. Excited to see us, he gathers us in his arms, hugging us tightly; if there is discomfort between him and our grandma, I don't notice. He loads us into the station wagon and takes us home, not to our familiar house with the large tree in the front yard but to a small two-bedroom apartment on the second floor, without a yard or a mother.

Dad didn't say anything about our mother's whereabouts, as far as I can recall.

I remember feeling sad, confused, and scared. That day I stepped onto the long road of taking the blame for her absence. No one corrected me because no one knew how I was feeling. No one thought or cared to ask. We did not see or hear from my mom for six months. Our parents divorced during the time she was gone.

To escape from the realities of life, books became my sanctuary. Withdrawing into fictional stories took me far away to safe worlds. I read everything I could get my hands on. You couldn't find me without a book in my hands. During my sophomore year of high school, I often ditched class and hid out in the school library. Nobody looks for a missing student in the school library, but I'm getting ahead of myself.

One book, though, *Dinky Hocker Shoots Smack*, by M.E. Kerr (Marijane Meaker), really resonated with me. As Dinky tried to get her mother's attention, I identified with her. Dinky's mother was so busy helping troubled teen drug addicts that she seemed to forget she had a teenage daughter of her own. When I read this book as a middle schooler, I was that daughter. What I remember most were the extremes Dinky went to get her mother's attention.

Growing up, I felt invisible—like I didn't belong, that I didn't fit in with my family or peers. I felt that everything I did wasn't quite right, was a little bit off. I was too loud, too happy, *too much*. I just wanted to fit in with my classmates. I wanted to be accepted and noticed by my parents—to feel like I mattered, that I had significance. Instead, I learned to keep to myself, to keep quiet and blend into the background so I wouldn't stand out, so no one would notice me.

I also have an unusual way of thinking, though I didn't know it at the time. I don't think in a straight line. My thoughts move more like a pinball, sometimes two, let loose in the machine. I also don't think outside of the box well. I draw conclusions more slowly than others. I *assumed* everyone thought like I did. My dad once told me a joke, and I didn't get it... for seven years. I didn't want to appear stupid or thick, so I pretended I understood at the time. But seven years later, that joke popped into my thoughts, and I got it. I laughed out loud, and I called my dad.

Over the many years I've been in the rooms of recovery, numerous people have shared the sentiment that, like me, they didn't feel like they fit in. They didn't feel like they belonged. Something felt off.

I think it would have been wonderful if I could have shared these emotions with my parents early on and been heard and understood. Identifying and expressing feelings was not a skill modeled in our home, so it was not a skill I learned. Subsequently, I entered adulthood ill-equipped to handle life on life's terms.

Living life on life's terms assumes one knows something about acceptance, accountability, responsibility, reliability, and a variety of other healthy responses that help us deal with circumstances as they occur—without overindulging or avoiding.

Instead, I attempted to *control all the outcomes*. I did my best to read the facial cues and sense the moods and responses of my parents in order to respond appropriately to survive. These skills served me well during my dad's second marriage.

Those first ten years of my life ended in confusion, uncertainty, and abrupt change. As a child, I had no lessons in dealing with the situations life handed me. No one gave me an instruction manual.

I've realized in reviewing those early years that I was subject to the whims of authority, that I had no freedom to choose and no autonomy. I felt like baggage, along for the ride, so to speak.

I did learn some valuable skills that served me well into adulthood, skills that helped me to survive what came next. Fortunately, or unfortunately, I used those skills so regularly that they became the rules rather than the exception. Those skills included avoiding emotional pain by escaping into distraction and fantasy, hoping for the best without much faith, reading a room to react accordingly, and being as quiet as possible to go unnoticed.

Grief was an emotion I knew well at a young age. The first thing I probably grieved was the loss of being the only child when my brother was born. The second grief experience was for lost friendships as a result of relocating. And the third most powerful event I grieved was my parent's dysfunctional and dissolved marriage. That last one also created the feeling that I was at fault or to blame, as if I was responsible for my mother's desertion. I felt guilt—in this case, feelings of deserving blame, especially for imagined offenses or from a sense of inadequacy—that I'd done something wrong but didn't know what that was, so I couldn't repair the damage. I had to live with it, and I carried that guilt, that self-blame, into my teens.

It's taken me years to address those unresolved issues, undo all those coping mechanisms, and more. Occasionally, I still slip into old habits when a circumstance brings up old memories. I use a set of techniques today to help me return to the present, to myself, and move forward in a healthier way. But at the age of nine, I did not have any techniques for moving through my feelings, so those feelings were bottled up.

Life got much worse before I was given the opportunity to process all that had happened in that brief final period of time when I was nine.

# CHAPTER TWO

## Domestic Warzone

Following the divorce, my dad, at just twenty-eight, did the best he could. From what I recall, before the divorce, he worked to provide and did minor yardwork while Mom oversaw housekeeping and childcare. After the divorce, Dad oversaw all things and didn't have much experience in the role Mom played. Between the ages of nine and almost eleven, my life was like drifting in a boat without oars across a dark, choppy sea.

The summer before the fourth grade was an early experience of living one day at a time. Our dad still had to make a living, and we were too young to be left home alone. He relied on the kindness of fellow members of his church, who were willing to care for us during the day while he was at work.

Dad asked a few church members for help with childcare. Our first caregiver was the wife of one of the church elders, a gentle woman with two young children of her own. We experienced a new culture in that home, as she was married to a Chinese man and ran her household in the Chinese tradition—shoes were removed upon entry, children were seen but not heard, and the husband was kind but showed little interest in us. This arrangement lasted a short while before Dad had to find another place for us to stay during those summer months.

The second family to volunteer had three sons. Two of the sons were our ages—seven and nine. They also had an older teenage son. When we stayed at their house, we hung out in their garage with the sons, reading comics and *MAD Magazine*. I heard my first Cheech and Chong and Dr. Demento radio programs in that garage. I also had my first encounter with an inappropriate older male.

One day the two younger boys asked me to visit their fort. It sounded like an adventure, so I said yes. Following them down the alley to another part of the neighborhood, we ended up in front of a garage that was propped halfway up. It was dark inside the garage, and as my eyes adjusted, I noticed a sheet hanging at the back of the garage suspended from an overhead storage cabinet. We ducked around the side of the sheet into the "fort." Behind the sheet was their older brother, who quickly maneuvered his way between me and the exit. A feeling of unease arose in me, and I wanted to leave the garage. The younger brothers were oblivious to the danger I sensed. The older brother stood menacingly between me and freedom.

I said aloud in what I hoped was a light and somewhat easy manner that I would like to leave. The older brother smiled and said, "But you just got here." Then he said I could leave if I gave him my panties. Shock and fear filled me. The younger brothers, surprised, began to protest but were cut off midsentence by the look he shot in their direction. Fearful now, I stated, more quietly, that I didn't want to give him my panties and that I'd like to leave. He again crooned, in a sweet, dangerous voice, that all I had to do was give him my panties, and I could leave. The two younger brothers seemed as terrified as I felt, and while they didn't leave me, they didn't intervene again. After a couple of attempts to escape, I finally gave in and gingerly, modestly removed my panties and tossed them toward him. He picked them up, threatened his brothers against telling on him and left the garage.

I was so relieved when he left that I cried. The brothers apologized, swore they had no idea he was there, and asked if I was okay. I was mortified about the entire experience and just wanted to forget it. I said, yeah, I'm fine. And we returned to their house. I never hung out in the garage again, though. And I never ever told my dad. I thought I was to blame. I shouldn't have gone to that garage, and I was afraid I'd be in trouble if I told him what had happened. I carried that secret for many years and used it as a ruler against most men in my future.

And then dad started seeing this woman.

My mother had returned to our lives, but I couldn't tell you when, and for a short time, we lived with her in Los Angeles. However, caring for us was too much for her, and she returned us to Dad.

While we were with Mom, Dad became reacquainted with a former co-worker, and they started dating. She had two children, both boys. She and Dad belonged to the same church. And Dad took us on many outings with her and her sons. Most of those outings ended in loud, angry fights between Dad and the other woman while we four kids continued our adventure, innocently pretending we didn't notice. Being in that woman's presence became increasingly uncomfortable, and I soon dreaded every visit. When she moved into our apartment complex, physically closer than ever, I was worried.

At age ten, another of those key moments occurred. One day my dad approached. He asked if he could talk with me. I don't remember the entire conversation, just the question he put to me after stating his case, "Do you think I should marry Ursula?"

It was a highly inappropriate question to ask a ten-year-old. I used to play that day back in my mind and change my answer. At the time, I deduced I must have done something that caused my mother to leave our home, to stop loving us. I told my dad, with my ten-year-old wisdom, that he should marry Ursula! Sage little girl that I was, I have to admit it wasn't entirely mirroring back what I knew he wanted to hear. Most of all, I didn't want to give my dad a reason to stop loving me, too. If I'd only known what was coming, I would have screamed no.

In Las Vegas, on December 31, 1975, my dad married Ursula. According to him, they fought on the plane ride home. His divorce from my mother was eighteen months old.

There aren't enough pages to recount all the messed-up mind games that woman played during the years she was married to my dad. Five years. As I transitioned from adolescence to puberty. As I wrote about this, my chest tightened, my body shook, tears formed in my eyes and rolled down my cheeks, and my face was aflush with emotion.

I never invited friends over. I was afraid for them to meet her until I realized she was gifted at pretending too. When meeting people, she wore a mask, a persona that was kind, nice, funny, and smiling. Back at home, alone with us, she was judgmental, belittling, spiteful, and had an iron fist about how the household had to be kept. Spotless, perfect, as if for show rather than to be lived in.

My sister was born at home in the fall of 1977, and we moved into a larger residence soon after. Family life got worse and physical violence between our parents began as well.

Held captive by that woman for hours during most weekends, she told me horrible, inappropriate detailed stories of her upbringing—of her own wicked stepmother and the torture she endured. She shared twisted personal memories of molestations and sexual experiences while lounging naked in the bathtub or sitting on the toilet. I was thirteen.

Our own mother was granted visitation rights which inadvertently put my brother and me between a rock and a hard place. Our stepmother expected us to call her Mom and became agitated when we called her by her name or spoke of our own mother. And when our mother came to pick us up, calling *her* Mom gave our stepmother an entire weekend to stew, cooking up some passive-aggressive retaliation for our return.

Trying to recall what it was like to live with Ursula and Dad as a couple, I can't remember him even being present except during their fights. I know he was, but in my memories... nothing. It was as if she erased him with her presence.

There was so much violence in our home that I withdrew as much as possible. It was never directed at us as long as we didn't engage, but we witnessed several physical altercations between our parents during the last two years of their marriage. The neighbors called the police on multiple occasions. I hid in my room as often as I could for self-preservation.

Living in that violent, turbulent home took its toll on all of us. My stepbrothers hated my dad, and I hated my stepmother. They solved disagreements with hand-to-hand combat; it was a lesson we took to heart one afternoon.

My older stepbrother said something to me, and I probably replied with some sarcastic retort. He called me out and asked me if I wanted to fight. The perfect storm. Because I'd been holding in too much for too long, I said, "Yeah." Our younger brothers—we each had one—followed us out to the garage.

Our garage was off-limits unless we were taking out the trash or doing laundry. We were not allowed to hang out in there, and we certainly weren't allowed to hold Fight Club in there. But that's exactly what we did. Four years of pent-up rage let loose in that garage that day between my stepbrother and me, while our brothers witnessed it from their safe vantage point on the washer and dryer.

I don't know who swung first or who swung last. I only remember a lot of hitting, kicking, and swearing, and also how good it felt to be letting it all out on someone who thought they could take it as much as I thought I could take it. I don't even know how long it lasted, but in the end, we lay on the floor of the garage, sweaty, dirty, and trying to catch our breath. I said something to him like, "Have you had enough?"

He replied, "Have you?"

We were sore and a little bruised, but we felt a million percent better, like letting all the steam out of a pressure cooker or releasing the cap on a shaken bottle of soda. We all headed back into the house, the fighting behind us, and resumed our lives as children.

During the last year of my dad's second marriage, I joined a youth group, the Junior Police Explorers. I'd been watching cop shows on television for a few years, and my career choice was to be a police officer. I wanted to become an undercover detective like Starsky and Hutch or a private detective like Jim Rockford, and I had to start somewhere. I spent my freshman year making friends and learning about what it took to become a police officer. I memorized the ten-code, and I exercised. I even volunteered to be a member of the color guard to carry our state flag in the Fourth of July parade that summer.

The uniform I wore to all the meetings and trainings was a loan from the group. One of the conditions of being accepted for another year in that group was that I purchase my own uniform. As a teenager without a job or a permit to get a job, I assumed my parents would buy my uniform. I was wrong. When the time came to put up the cash for a uniform, my dad informed me that if I wanted the uniform, I would have to pay for it myself. I was aghast. I argued that I didn't have the money and I didn't have a job. He proceeded to list all the jobs I could do that didn't require a job permit, including mowing lawns, walking dogs, and babysitting. I was livid inside, tears rolling down my face. *It was so unfair!* I thought. Refusing to risk possible rejection from neighbors, I didn't ask if I could walk their dogs or mow their lawns. I quit the police explorers instead and blamed my dad. For years I thought, *If only he'd helped me out, I'd have been a police officer instead of taking the turn I took.*

I understand today that he did the right thing, asking me to pay for the uniform myself. I could have heard that months earlier, though, instead of when I needed the money. I also didn't know then that he simply could not afford the uniform's cost. The lesson was valid; the timing was terrible.

Near the end of that year, yet another critical moment occurred, setting the stage for a path I'd later regret. Again, it was in the summer months, right before my sophomore year of high school. Have you ever woken from a dream only to discover you were still asleep but now in a nightmare? I woke from a disturbing dream to a frightening reality. Ursula was pounding on me with her fists, screaming obscenities into my face, literally spitting mad. She was fiercely angry, and I, being roused from a dead sleep, was disoriented. I crawled to the farthest corner of my bed, putting distance between her flailing fists and my body. I don't remember any of her words, but the venom of her mood was terrifying. It seemed she and my father had had another fight, and she lost her shit. I became the target of her vengeance.

She concluded her insane rant with the words, "Get ready for school, or you'll be late!"

*Yeah, right.*

Sitting in that corner for several minutes, catching my breath, I decided what I'd do next. I grabbed my backpack and pulled out all my school supplies. I filled that backpack with what seemed logical items for running away. I'd had enough!

While I was stuffing t-shirts and underpants into my bag, the older of my two stepbrothers peeked into my room and asked me what I was doing. Hesitating only briefly, I told him what had happened and that I was out of there. An afterthought was that he might tell his mom, but his only response was, "Can I come too?"

We ran away that day and, by evening, had walked several miles with no real plan. After a little discussion, he decided we could call his dad.

We spent two weeks at his dad's house in Torrance, California. His dad had called my dad to let him know what was going on, and surprisingly my dad was okay with my staying there awhile. Eventually, though, I had to go home. Upon arrival, my stepmother chastised and criticized and accused me of many lies she made up about the kind of houseguest I was while staying at her ex-husband's home. I sat stoically. I took the brunt of her words, and I said nothing. However, something began brewing inside me. Something that started the morning she battered me with her fists—the morning I decided to leave. Eventually, she finished her criticism of my perceived behavior. I went back to my room.

School resumed, and fall was upon us. One afternoon when my brother and I returned from school, our dad's car was in the driveway, which was odd, considering it was only three o'clock. We stood in the kitchen and heard Dad upstairs in his room, sobbing loudly. This terrified me more than I can tell you. He didn't come downstairs for a long time, hours. When he did, he told us that our stepmother was gone, that she had taken her sons and our little sister with her. We didn't see Dad again for a couple of days. He quit his job as a salesman and got a job as a cab driver, so he could be home during the day for us. In my fifteen-year-old mind, all the events from 1975 until 1981 were on me. I believed I was to blame. If only I'd told my dad no when he asked about marrying Ursula. But it was done, and because of me—I told myself once again—everything in our lives changed.

Five years spent in a hostile environment was much like living in a war zone. Shell-shocked from repeated surprise attacks, making and remaking alliances with unreliable sources, and literally fending for myself daily with no one I could trust in my POW camp. I didn't even have alliances with outside forces, such as the other parent, teachers, or other adult figures. That summer, even my best friend turned on me. I felt completely alone in my environment. Following the departure of my stepmother and her children, being left with a broken man we called Dad, something began to emerge inside me, a sense of power in the most primal form. The summer of my fifteenth year was an awakening into defiance.

# CHAPTER THREE

# Coming of Age

In looking back, I realize the first substance I used to escape was not marijuana—it was alcohol. My dad gave me a sip of his beer when I was nine or so. It tasted wonderful, refreshing, tangy, and bitter. I don't think he expected me to like it.

On my friend's fourteenth birthday, her dad gave five of us a beer to share. I felt emboldened. I thought being an adult felt like that. There was also a feeling of excitement. An *adult* gave us a beer to celebrate our friend. We were children, and an adult permitted us to drink. It was all the invitation I needed.

It didn't take long—just weeks afterward—before I stole my first beer from the poolside bar that belonged to another friend's dad. During a sleepover, when everyone else was inside, I stole the beer and guzzled it surreptitiously in the backyard. Alone, with an entire beer to myself this time, I dropped into an altered state. I felt giddy, lighter, and dangerous because I'd gotten away with something. I felt free.

Following the departure of my stepmother and my father's withdrawal from life, I began acting out. I ditched class regularly, and I skipped school often. During the summer between my freshman and sophomore years, a boy I liked convinced me to join him in "borrowing" his mother's car. In a surreal twist, the event turned into grand theft auto, and within forty-eight hours, we got caught. But his mom didn't press charges, which led us to steal the same car again a couple of weeks later. We were arrested within hours, and this time she pressed charges—on me. I was removed from my father's custody, made a ward of the court, placed in the juvenile court system, and finally in a group home—a county residence program designed to rehabilitate troubled teens.

While living in that first group home, I followed the rules and flew under the radar. I was troubled, yes, but I was placed in a home with some girls much more troubled than me. I tried to fit in, to get along, but the oldest girl in that house had been in the system for a while. At face value, she seemed kind and protective, but she showed her true colors—spiteful, manipulative, mean-spirited—late at night when the group home parents went to bed. It was like living with a younger version of my stepmother.

After my first few weeks there, for instance, she looked at me over the breakfast table one morning and said, "You're so pretty. Have you ever worn make-up?" Soon she was performing a make-over. I was grateful for the attention and the implied friendship I thought was taking place. I felt pretty when she was done, and the other girls thought I looked good. Apparently, too good. I remember the look on her face when the other girls praised me. I assume she felt threatened, and soon she was tearing me down, calling me names and accusing me of thinking I was better than the rest of them. All four other girls sided with her. Already insecure with my position in life, I was confused, hurt and scared.

We were required to attend school during the summer months and took public transportation to get there. Carrying a backpack filled with my most precious personal belongings instead of my schoolbooks, I snuck out the back door and used that same public transportation to head back to my own neighborhood. I ran away. Back with my own friends, I overindulged in beer with some older kids. Of course, I threw up. It didn't take long for the police to find me. I think a parent turned me in. Arrested for violating probation and breaking curfew—I was a minor, after all—I was shuffled back to that same group home via juvenile hall.

Avoiding the attention of the other girls, I kept to myself, doing my chores and going to school. The garage had a pay phone, and I called my boyfriend often. One evening, after a call that led me to believe he had another girlfriend, I took to the garage's roof for peace and escape with a pint of peppermint schnapps. I can't remember how I procured that bottle, but I do remember the drink tasted sweet and refreshing, like Christmas with a kick. The feelings of betrayal and abandonment drifted away.

Restless, irritable and discontent, I didn't want to be in that group home anymore. One evening the group home parents drove us to a house in North Orange County for a group therapy session. Seizing my chance, I crawled out the bathroom window, found a bus stop and headed back to my neighborhood again. I spent a couple of weeks on the lam that time, hanging out with various friends and on one very nice boat in Huntington Harbor. I even made an unbelievable amount of money for my age by providing my security services at a three-day harvest carnival. The manager was not very discerning. However, I was spotted again during the carnival, which was hosted by the police department, and returned to juvenile hall once more.

Well, running away a second time only served to anger the judge who'd sent me to the group home in the first place, and he placed me in another group home—sixty miles away—in Riverside County.

It was early September 1980. Heading into a new school year in a completely foreign environment, once again keeping my head low, I dressed in army fatigues with my army surplus backpack slung over my shoulders, bangs hanging over my eyes. I knew no one but the girls in my group home, and I did not trust them. I was a minority in my group home and in the high school, being one of the few white girls in the student population and the only one back at the house. You might be thinking, "Poor, little white girl, a minority? How sad." My race didn't matter; what mattered was I was the only one like me. An African American woman ran the house with no sympathy for me, and it housed three Mexican girls, an Italian and another black girl. Conflict was present from the moment I arrived. I was naïve and scared. I didn't know how to behave around these ethnicities. I offended someone every day. One of the girls, my roommate, was a gangbanger from Watsonville. She took pity on me, showed kindness, and helped me navigate this new situation, telling me how to act and what to say.

This group home had a counselor who visited weekly, intending to rehabilitate us. The first couple of visits were okay, but meeting with her became redundant. Once again, I was interacting with an adult who didn't want to seek the truth. She only wanted to hear what she wanted to hear, which was me lying about how I ended up in that home in the first place. During several of the sessions with her, I requested that she include my dad in those talks, that my issues were with him, and it might benefit us both if we could talk it out with a neutral third party. Time and time again, she disagreed. I decided enough was enough, and I devised a cunning plan to get myself thrown out of the group home and returned to juvenile hall.

I requested a Bic razor from the group home mother on the pretense that I'd like to shave. I actually intended to harm myself so she would see that I needed to be locked up. I discovered that breaking apart a Bic razor was nearly impossible, but only nearly. I wrestled the sharp, metal blades free of their plastic prison. I walked into my group home mother's room and proceeded to slice long grooves into my left forearm, dripping red blood into her white shag carpet. I explained that I wanted to return to jail. She was not happy about my tactic, and she did not respond as I had hoped. My punishment was grounding, sent to my room to think about my actions and a special visit with the counselor.

A month later, in late October, I ran away with another boy, who was also in a group home, and his friend. Instead of taking the bus home after school, we just started walking. On the second or third night, in an empty dwelling of a new housing development, one of them produced what he called a joint. I gave it a try. It was the first time I smoked marijuana, and it was terrifying. The joint was tainted, laced with something dangerous, like phencyclidine, maybe. We all suffered horrible hallucinations. The next day I decided that if marijuana did that, I wasn't ever smoking it again.

We were on the run, wandering around Riverside County for a couple of weeks. Tired of sleeping out in the cold, hungry most of the time, I called my mother one evening from a pay phone in front of a convenience store, hoping she would help me. Admittedly, it was a last resort. I was surprised to discover that she hadn't known I'd even run away. I'd been on the run for two weeks, and my mom didn't know? She told me she would help, though, and I read her the address of my location off of the telephone. One of the boys was still with me and was uneasy about this turn of events, but I reassured him that my mom was cool and would want to help us. However, twenty minutes later, a police car pulled up in front of the store, and two police officers got out of the car. I truly believed it was a coincidence that they were just stopping at the store to grab a snack. Imagine my surprise when one of them turned to me and said my name. I felt anger, betrayal and defeat. I had never felt less loved by my mother than I did at that moment. My fifteen-year-old self could not fathom why she called the cops instead of coming to rescue me herself.

I began shifting the blame I'd been carrying onto others. If this, then that. And none of the future results were going to be on me. I became adept at logically assigning blame where it was truly due—on my parents, my brother, my teachers, my friends.

While my probation officer tried to figure out what to do with me next, I spent my fifteenth Christmas and my sixteenth birthday in juvenile hall. Apparently, she couldn't put me in another home or a mental hospital—yes, that was an option—without my permission once I turned sixteen. Every time we met, I expressed my desire to return to my father's custody and every time, she told me that was not an option. Eventually, though, I wore her down, and I was returned to my home. In a strange turn of events, I was released from probation following a shoplifting event; my probation officer told me that she'd had enough, that in her eyes, my probation violation was a sign that I wasn't interested in being a member of society, and that my plan was not going to work. She signed the order releasing me right then. I was stunned. I also decided to drop out of high school, get a job, and become an adult. That was another short-lived venture because I lived my life after high school in the moment. I didn't think about the future or consider the consequences of my actions. I followed the crowd that accepted me, and that usually started with a boy.

# CHAPTER FOUR

## From Magic to Madness

A final pivotal moment in my life draws a distinct line between before I used drugs and alcohol and what came after. I don't remember the details so much as the feelings. I distinctly remember that I wasn't drinking very often before this event and didn't smoke marijuana.

At eighteen, I lived with a boyfriend in the truck tire repair shop where he worked. I was timid, quiet, and agreeable. I did not know what I needed or wanted, having learned the life lesson of going with the flow to keep everybody else happy. My boyfriend was good-looking and seemed tough and cool—think Danny Zucko from Grease—and I felt special most of the time. I felt grown-up.

And then I got pregnant.

I wasn't using birth control and never asked my partners to. Why? Making that request required that I stand up for myself, show some backbone, and risk severing our bond. My training did not include those skills, and my self-esteem at that time was fragile, barely existent.

The result of my choice was an unwanted pregnancy. I was afraid to tell him, but eventually, I had to. I felt ashamed to be repeating my parents' mistakes. I decided to terminate the pregnancy. I never considered talking with him about keeping the baby, and at eighteen, I was not prepared or willing to have a child, with or without his help.

My mother, the same woman I'd hated for calling the police when I reached out for help, went with me, and may even have paid the clinic. Did the baby's father show up as well? I believe he did that first time. Following the procedure, I moved to my dad's instead of returning to the shop. I remember feeling a great deal of self-pity and humiliation.

Weeks later, I agreed to see the boyfriend again.

We met at the pier in Newport Beach, along with his friend who had introduced us and that guy's girlfriend. My boyfriend had a huge bottle of tequila in one hand. The four of us sat on the edge of the pier carrying on awkward, superficial conversation, the sun setting behind us, feet dangling over the sand, passing the bottle until we blotted out the awkward and resumed our lives, living in the moment, not considering the consequences of our actions.

I could not afford the procedure that included sedation, and that night on the pier, I couldn't drink enough or smoke enough to erase the physical pain. The emotional pain always lingered near the surface as much as I tried to bury those feelings deep under a sea of booze and pretend it hadn't happened. The emotional ache—a heavy burden of guilt from the abortion procedure—is still present.

Shortly after the meeting at the pier, I returned to the tire repair shop, and soon after that, we had a fight. His boss had requested some "services" from me while my boyfriend was out on a job. My boyfriend was upset because I would not provide those services to his employer. I was hurt and angry.

It was very late in the evening when I made the next decision. I knew some other guys who also lived at the shop smoked weed. Leaving my room on the pretense of using the toilet, I bee-lined it to their bedroom door instead. I knocked lightly at first. No answer. Not to be deterred, I knocked again, a little more loudly. The red-headed guy opened the door, looking a little annoyed and half-asleep until he focused on my face. Then a smile lit up his face. I smiled back and asked him if he had some weed he was willing to share. I did not consider how late it was or that they had to work the next day. My only concern was to get what I wanted. I got high, and it was magic. The redhead and I laughed a bit and flirted a little. What started as an act of spite to show my boyfriend I didn't need him ended in discovering that I felt better than I had before the fight and didn't care what he thought anymore.

The second I smoked pot, everything suddenly tumbled into place. Instantaneously, an ease came over me like a blanket. For perhaps the first time ever, I could speak to others effortlessly. My words just said themselves. Suddenly, I felt comfortable, no longer self-conscious. I felt attractive, people laughed at my sense of humor, and I didn't have to work at it. Maybe I was attractive and funny without marijuana, but I didn't know it. I was too up in my head when I was straight. When I was high, I felt the belonging I sought; it didn't concern me what other people thought of me.

After the effect inevitably wore off, my discomfort returned, I again cared what other people thought, and I wanted to be invisible. I worried about what my parents, the cool kids, siblings, and friends were thinking about me, and I'd conclude I needed more of that fearless, confident feeling that weed provided to fit comfortably in the world.

I truly believed that no one else felt like they didn't belong—never making the connection that everyone I hung out with probably felt out of place because, eventually, everyone I hung out with smoked weed.

The result of my pretending that we hadn't gotten pregnant and I hadn't had an abortion was that I got pregnant again, by the same man, with the same result—another unwanted pregnancy. Sedated for the procedure that second time made the incident more dream-like, like it hadn't happened. The relationship with that boyfriend ended shortly after the abortion. I kept seeing alcohol and weed, though.

A few months passed, and I'd gotten a job as a receptionist and "gofer" at a law office. I borrowed my boss's car to run office errands, and one day I spotted the boy who was with me the day I'd called my mom for help. He stood on a corner near my office, waiting for the light to change. He needed a ride home, and I offered to drive. Back at his house, we ended up getting high, and I lost track of time. I returned my boss's car the following day and was fired.

I wasn't worried, though. I'd met a bunch of people who lived in a motel near that boy's house who subscribed to my philosophy of living in the moment. I moved in, which in reality meant that I just never left, couch surfing from motel room to motel room with a bunch of other twenty-somethings who didn't want to live life on life's terms. I thought I'd found the perfect life, doing what I wanted, drinking, getting high. I was grateful that no one expected much from me. For a while, I landed with a mother and her three children, and all I had to do was help keep the small room clean and watch her youngest child occasionally.

Almost everyone who lived in that motel smoked weed. Eventually, all the people I associated with drank and smoked. Marijuana was everywhere I was, and I loved it.

Choosing that path had consequences, but I couldn't see them at the time. I had little job experience and limited education. I hadn't seen or spoken to my parents in months. I was not progressing in life.

I was developing a hell of a cannabis habit, though, always politely prodding someone to light up and share. I found another eligible guy to hang around who always seemed to have weed. That he had a girlfriend was not a concern. He dreamed of being a professional boxer.

I had one little problem, however. In order to get high, I still bummed weed off other people. My marijuana habit grew like a hungry beast, always needing more. The people around me were not smoking it frequently enough for me.

Sometimes I look back on my life and wonder how I lived this long. I routinely put myself in dangerous situations. One instance was when I was hanging out with the future boxer and some of his friends, smoking weed. He chopped up a few lines of white powder on a glass picture frame with a single-edge razor blade and handed me a straw after he'd snorted a line. I quickly reasoned that I'd never done cocaine, but I'd seen enough of it on television to assume that this little bit wouldn't harm me, and besides, he seemed okay. Naively believing the guy handing me the straw had my best interests at heart, I accepted it and snorted up that white powder. The next sensation was like shards of glass lacerating my sinuses, and this thought popped into my head, *So this is how I die, eighteen years old, in a stranger's motel room.* A look of sincere concern came over the face of the future boxer, and he asked if I'd ever done speed before. Although I never had, I probably tried to act like I had. He reassured me that I'd be okay and called me "Crazy Girl." He'd call me that a lot over the next several years.

Another time, I needed weed, my own weed. I was tired of waiting for others to light up. I'd had a fight with the future boxer and was in a spiteful "I'll show him" mood. I remembered that the future boxer had scored some weed from an old biker dude who lived in an apartment garage near the motel, so I went on a quest to find weed. It was late in the evening, after ten o'clock, and I couldn't remember which garage the dealer lived in. I spent time knocking on several garage doors before I found the right one. We didn't know each other, but I had a name that we both knew. I left that garage a while later, alive and high, with a bag of my very own weed. I don't think I even had any money. I got a front, saying, "I'll gladly pay you Tuesday for a bit of weed today." I didn't need anyone anymore. I could get high on my own.

There were many times following my late-night alley adventure to score weed that could have cost me my life, yet, here I am writing about it, alive today by the grace of a power greater than me.

The future boxer and I made up. He got a job working in a warehouse, I got a job working in an amusement park, and we rented our very own room at the motel. Things between us went well for a while, and then I got pregnant. I quit my job in a second and applied for state aid. I was nineteen.

He and I married in November. Our daughter was born in March 1985. We were separated by September, and eventually, we divorced. I expected him to change into my preconceived idea of a family man overnight, but he didn't live up to my ideal of a husband or a father.

I spent the next few years as a working, single mom, jumping from one man to another, looking for the Hollywood illusion of love, and maintaining my high.

# CHAPTER FIVE

# A Progressive Disease

**INSIDIOUS, adjective** *in·sid·i·ous* | \ in-ˈsi-dē-əs \
**Definition of insidious,** from Webster's New World College Dictionary, Fifth Edition
**2:** working harm in a slow or subtle manner; hence, more dangerous than seems evident (*an insidious disease*)

Let me tell you a story. It's a parable for marijuana addiction and its insidious nature. It's about a boat with a tiny hole in its hull, lower than the water line, just under the steering mechanism. The captain notices something is wrong because a puddle of water eventually forms at the bottom of the boat. Doing a little investigating, he finds the hole. *It's small,* he tells himself, *and it's just a little bit of water, not even enough to bail out.* So, for a while, he ignores it. Eventually, the puddle is ankle-deep; grabbing a nearby tin cup, he starts bailing out the water, valiantly trying to get rid of it.

Time goes by, six months, and he keeps ladling water up and pouring it over the side of the boat. The sun and the seawater wear on the hole, and it widens. Now the captain uses a small metal bucket, but he still does nothing about the hole. Another six months pass, and the hole continues to grow. One night he docks the boat, and the next morning when he returns, his boat is underwater.

That's what marijuana addiction is like, a subtle progression. One day we're just having fun with our friends, and the next, we're underwater.

It took a long time before I found myself underwater, starting to drown.

The first time I quit smoking pot was in 1987 to attend a six-month certification program for production art. I quit smoking cold turkey. No help, no program, no problem. Wanting to do well so I could get a good job and provide for my daughter, I stayed clean and sober for the entire six-month program. But, at the end of the program, the instructor invited all the students out for congratulatory drinks, and that drink led to a joint which got me started again. I'd finished the course successfully, which justified "earning" that drink, that smoke.

I didn't have a problem with marijuana. Marijuana was just a symptom. I had a problem with my thinking.

Along the way, from my first drink to my last dance with "Mary Jane," were a slew of warning signs that I ignored. Remember, I didn't have the tools to function as a healthy adult, and *I didn't know* I didn't have the tools. I managed to scrape by often enough, and getting by was good enough for me. I provided for myself and eventually provided for my daughter.

Upon completing that course, I landed my first graphic designer gig as a typesetter in a print shop.

"I think I have a problem with marijuana." This is what I told my boss in 1988.

While working in a printing shop, setting up all the artwork, I discovered the press operator smoked marijuana because one day, he asked me if I did. Of course, I said yes.

That first job lasted almost a year, during which I smoked weed most days after work. Never before or during. That would come later. But at that time, I guess I still had some standards.

I started making mistakes at work though, and smoking more weed at home. Not just on the weekends or a couple of nights a week, but every night. And something in me at the ripe old age of twenty-three told me that maybe I smoked too much. I was forgetting things. Maybe someone I knew had said something to me about it. I don't recall. Thinking I might have a problem and I should talk to someone, one morning I asked my boss about it. I told him that I thought I had a problem with marijuana. His response was not what I needed to hear, but it was certainly what I wanted to hear, "Nobody has a problem with marijuana." He laughed a little when he said it, and he looked annoyed. Since he was a business owner, a father, and my boss, I figured he was probably right, and I let it rest.

I smoked for nine more years before I gave it another thought. I didn't see the signs that indicated I might have a problem. Signs like continuing to smoke progressively more and more weed, always high when I wasn't working, often high when I was, and hanging out with people I knew used marijuana. On top of it, I drank during work hours.

Marijuana is often referred to as the gateway drug, and my use put me in circles with people who also used speed and cocaine, people willing to share for a time.

If anyone else saw the red flags, they weren't saying anything to me.

A three-year cycle of hardcore addiction began in 1989, starting with a cocaine habit that became more important than anything else in my life. My daughter lived with me, and on her fourth birthday, a friend called to tell me he scored an eight-ball—an eighth of an ounce, about three and a half grams of cocaine. The moments following that call are mostly a blur, but I remember the tunnel-vision—get the "blow;" that was the only goal, above everything else. Knowing my ex-husband was on his way to pick up our daughter, I asked my roommate to watch her until he arrived. Leaving my house on a single-minded mission, I blew by my Dad as he walked up the sidewalk toward our apartment. I can remember the surprised, confused look on his face. He'd shown up to celebrate his grand daughter's birthday. Did I even invite him? I don't remember. Giving him some lame excuse, I never slowed down. I'll never be able to take back those moments or tell this story without feeling deep guilt. That's where addiction took me. I cared for nothing and no one if they got between me and my drugs.

My cocaine use was momentarily interrupted by a car accident. I rear-ended a vehicle on the on-ramp of a freeway on my way home from scoring cocaine, knocking the wind out of me and popping out the windshield of my van. The driver of the car I hit got out of his car and came back to check on me. He took one look at my face as I struggled to catch my breath, hightailed it back to his car and took off. Police showed up, and I expected to be arrested and hauled away to jail. Physically, I looked okay, but my van was out of commission and towed away. The police released me, and I walked the six miles home, fueled by the cocaine I still had on me, grateful they hadn't found it. The incident scared me enough to take a break from that drug for a while. I had two or three more rounds with cocaine in the years after that, knowing that bad news would follow every time I snorted that first line. I certainly know I was bad news when I got near it, but addiction is a power all its own, and I believed I was powerless against it.

Addiction took me from cocaine to crack and eventually to methamphetamines. I was drawn to these stimulants and the people who dealt them, not because I enjoyed the people or the drugs but because of an overwhelming and uncontrollable craving. The drugs fed the pleasure receptors in my brain. Overrode the danger signs. A stronger desire for more followed those short-lived bursts of euphoria.

Marijuana was always the solution to the cocaine problem or the speed problem, or the alcohol problem. Weed slowed me down, mellowed me out, and saved me from myself. As bad as my experiences got, they could have been so much worse.

How did I pull myself out of that deep stimulant abyss? Divine intervention, perhaps, brought about by a series of circumstances. An alarm in my brain brayed loud enough to pierce through the veil of addiction. Ultimately, miraculously, my daughter's need for a mother contributed to pulling myself out of that particular addiction.

Being an addict—knowing the feeling of powerlessness, of being incapable of saying no when drugs or alcohol were offered—I can say that marijuana brought on the same selfish, self-centered thoughts and feelings that the other, harder drugs did. The fall from marijuana was a slower, softer one than the hard and fast landing that accompanied cocaine, crack or meth.

Marijuana was still quite prevalent, but I was able—with the help of some more grounded individuals—to put the stimulants behind me for a time. When the quality of those surrounding me improved, so did I.

Once again, though, I met a man. I created a fantasy about this man, seeing only what I wanted to see, and I entered into another relationship. Once again, I became pregnant.

While I was pregnant, I abstained from all harmful substances. That pregnancy led to my second marriage in 1992. Again, a poor decision ... agreeing to marriage. I wanted desperately to say no, but the fear of raising two children on my own without financial security sealed that deal. Instead, I married, and his two children, my daughter and the son we had together, created an instant family.

That second marriage lasted twenty years. Ten years into the marriage, I got arrested and chose sobriety over prison.

Looking back, my last years of using were pitiful. All outward appearances fulfilled the illusion that I had it all together; I worked in the corporate headquarters of a large healthcare company for the general counsel, drove a minivan, and dressed professionally. However, on the inside, I was lonely, depressed most of the time, and suicidal—my home life was in chaos.

As a parent, I wasn't a great role model. I lived in a bubble and would not take responsibility for my role. I was doing my best to avoid feelings of inadequacy and hopelessness while keeping up the impression of a perfectly wonderful life. I'd taken on much more than I could manage, and my answer was always to be high and drink when I could. Following a particularly wild roller coaster of a year that included the return of methamphetamine, my stepdaughter left us to live with her mother permanently in 1997.

She never returned from a summer visit. I was packing her belongings and living in perpetual denial; I was unprepared for a letter I found in her belongings, written to someone else. Of course, I read it, and my heart became heavier and heavier as I read the words I could have written about my own stepmother. She wrote, and I paraphrase, *"I never do enough. I tried my best to be helpful and do well, but I can't keep up with all the tasks she gives me. I don't think she loves me."* She thought I didn't love her. I thought I showed I did.

I knew what she was talking about, though. I was constantly rattling off five and six things at a time I wanted the children to complete and expecting them to remember all of it. Since I often used methamphetamines during that particular period, it's a wonder that I didn't expect more. The number of my demands—and they were demands—were unreasonable for children. But in my mind, from my skewed perspective, I was just asking them to do what I would do myself. It never occurred to me I was being unreasonable. Looking back, I was out of my mind most of the time.

Where did I cross the line from having fun, blowing off steam, and relaxing to the place where I couldn't and wouldn't function without alcohol and drugs?

I don't know. It's a progressive disease, addiction, and I progressed.

When did I begin to see I had a problem dealing with life but wasn't ready to shed light on that problem and begin to seek help?

Again, I couldn't tell you. Life became a blur after a while.

I promised myself so many times that the next joint would be my last, and the next morning I'd be rolling another joint or loading another bowl. By 2001, I felt a great deal of self-loathing whenever I smoked. I had called a recovery support group, and my excuse to continue using was that the voicemail message was so long it gave me time to roll a bunch of joints while I waited to leave a message.

I smoked marijuana for twenty years. I come back to marijuana because it was the last thing I gave up before getting clean and sober. I didn't believe I had a problem with it. I didn't know it was a depressant. I did know that in the beginning, I loved how I felt when I was high and didn't like how I felt when I wasn't.

Am I a marijuana addict? I am. If you are asking yourself if you might be a marijuana addict, I ask you this, can you identify with anything in my story so far?

If you relate to anything in my story, I encourage you to read on and decide for yourself if you are a marijuana addict.

# CHAPTER SIX

## Am I A Marijuana Addict?

No one could decide for me or tell me I was an addict. I will tell you that if anyone had ever suggested to me that I might smoke too much marijuana, I would have disagreed. I believed I could quit anytime I wanted—I just didn't want to. For three years before I quit smoking, I visited a therapist every two or three weeks. This therapist brought up the subject of my marijuana use a few times, and every time, I assured him that weed was not my problem—my problem was my boss, my spouse, my kids, my friends, and my life circumstances. Surely not marijuana.

How would *you* answer the question? My answer changed over time from no to maybe and, finally, to yes.

Only we get to decide if we have a problem with weed.

After our daughter's move back to her mother's home, we were threatened with eviction if we didn't choose to move.

In a new home, a small apartment in a large complex, I began crying while watching heart-tugging television commercials. I'd see a commercial, start crying, and before I knew it, I was sobbing uncontrollably. I was scaring myself and my second husband.

You know, it's funny—not ha ha funny, but sad really—when I was around thirteen or fourteen years old, I spent the night at a friend's house and we watched a television movie about Harry Houdini starring Paul Glaser. I knew the story, but at the end, when Harry died in that most tragic way, the tears started flowing, and I couldn't stop them then either. I was embarrassed and went to the bathroom to try and calm myself down. I couldn't. I would almost get it under control, and then it would start up again. I was in that bathroom for probably ninety minutes, my friend checking on me every once in a while. I scared her, and I scared myself. As an adult, I understood that the movie triggered feelings I'd been holding in check as best as I could. It seems that moving into that new apartment triggered the same response.

Around this same period, our pot dealer moved away. To another state. I think the dealer moving away was probably the Universe intervening. We'd been buying our marijuana from him for years, and at that time, it was hard to find a reliable dealer. Today a person can go to a store, a dispensary, and purchase marijuana in all its forms. Maybe a few private dealers still grow weed in their yards and sell it out of their homes, but when I was smoking pot, that was the *only* way to get it. From a dealer.

I'm pretty sure my husband and I mutually decided to quit smoking pot rather than find another dealer. We did have a friend we hit up once to score weed, but that turned into a scene, and we chose sobriety for a while. Again, without a program. No support. Still a secret, but at least I wasn't using. That period of clean time lasted a little over a year.

Without weed, I still practiced inappropriate behaviors. We still drank periodically, and we had a neighbor who occasionally parked his car in our carport without our permission. It pissed me off. Serving my own form of justice, I took it upon myself one evening to teach that person a lesson. Did alcohol fuel my decision? Well, I had a drink in my hand when I went out to do the deed. Beer in one hand, large nail in the other, I knelt down in the shadows near the car's rear tire, intending to push the tire valve, releasing all the air. That'd show them! Just as I got the air flowing, I was startled by my older son.

"What are you doing?" he asked.

"Teaching this guy a lesson about parking in our space," was my reply.

My son pointed out that if I let the air out of the tires, the car's owner would never be able to move it. Sigh. He was right. I felt foolish—for getting caught and for not seeing the obvious outcome. I did shit like that a lot.

Until July 1999, I was weed-free. Drinking beers in the parking lot before a concert provided the lubricant, a slippery slope when an opportunity presented itself. During the concert, someone passed a joint down the aisle. My excitement grew as the smoldering joint came closer and closer. Handed to me, I took a hit, and it was game on.

By the oddest of coincidences, the pot dealer who had moved away moved back to town shortly after that concert. Finding excuses to meet the dealer, I scored and smoked secretly for several weeks. Smoking again, in secret, killed my appetite, and I shed a noticeable amount of weight before I found a clever and manipulative way to include my husband in the reawakening of the marijuana beast.

After a while, though, self-loathing arose whenever I lit up, and I began to regret my decision to smoke and include my husband. Once again, I saw smoking marijuana as a problem. One I couldn't put down when I wanted to put it down.

In 2000, when I discovered my teenagers were also smoking weed, I smoked with them, thinking it would be a good way to bridge the generation gap. That was my actual thought, and I worked to convince my husband of my sound logic. I became like that parent who allowed their kids to drink at home because "the kids were gonna drink anyway," and at least the parents would know their kids were safe. That brilliant plan, smoking with my teens and their friends, lasted about six months, and I felt worse than ever. Smoking together ended when I ran out of weed, and I mentioned it to my fifteen-year-old son, who brought me a joint. I took it, and I smoked it, and I cried. I stopped smoking with them but still wasn't ready to change my behavior.

Was I a marijuana addict?

My mother, a member of a twelve-step recovery program for several years, would know, I reasoned. Calling her, I explained what was happening and asked, "Do you think I'm a marijuana addict?" I expected to get a nice clear-cut answer, like when my boss told me that nobody has a problem with marijuana.

But I did not expect what she said next.

"Honey, I can't answer that for you. Only you can decide." I was confused. She continued, "If you only smoke on an occasional Saturday night and don't think about it the next day or all week, then you might not be an addict. If you smoke consistently and find you are experiencing problems in other areas of your life that might be related to your marijuana use, you might be an addict. I can't decide for you, though."

In case you're wondering, I didn't decide. I kept smoking, feeling miserable. But I began abstaining, quitting a few days at a time. I started telling my husband and a few using friends I was giving it up. My resolve lasted a few days before I started using again.

You may have heard this definition of insanity, doing the same thing over and over again, expecting different results. I believed each time I picked up again would be different than the last mile, that this time I would control my use. In the end, I was smoking marijuana on the way to work, feeling defeated after the first hit, and throwing the pipe and the weed out the window onto the freeway, only to call my dealer on the way home. This insanity lasted about a year.

The last mind- and mood-altering substance I quit was marijuana. Remember, weed led me to the places where I found other drugs. Those stronger drugs had a stronger pull. Marijuana, however—now, that was a slower burn, like incense. Light a stick of incense, and it takes a long time to burn from one end of the stick to the other. Light the fuse in a stick of dynamite and run because that fuse burns fast and leaves a powerful mess behind. *Ka-boom.* Marijuana was eventually the only thing I thought I needed. And then marijuana turned on me, too. It was no longer fun or joyful.

I was filled with despair whenever I smoked. I wanted to quit, and I couldn't.

Early one morning in February of 2003, I reported a burglary at my home. To my surprise, I was arrested for felony cultivation. Someone had broken into our house and stolen from us, and I wanted justice. However, I was also growing a marijuana plant on my patio. I learned that day that growing any amount of marijuana in California at that time was illegal. I sat in a jail cell most of the day and overheard another detainee talking on the phone to her friend about the "sad, old lady in the next cell." Me, the sad, old lady, at thirty-eight.

I'd been seeking an answer, a way to quit. I mean, why else would I throw pot out the window of my car into the freeway fast lane time and time again? Or tell people I was quitting? Well, unexpectedly, the Universe provided that answer. And my arrest charge had to be *big* because a slap on the hand wouldn't work. I know that about me. The felony promised me one to three years in prison if I was convicted.

Part of my court requirement—if I didn't want a felony on my record—was that I participate in a PC 1000 diversion program.

The program, Penal Code 1000 or PC 1000 for short, is a deferred judgment program for first-time drug offenders. I agreed to participate in an eighteen-month program that included diversion classes—ten three-hour classes where I would learn about addiction and recovery, as well as submit to drug testing to prove I hadn't been using marijuana—while continuing to abide by the law. No drinking or drugging until the eighteen-month program was concluded. I was also required to attend twelve-step meetings and get a little blue court card signed to prove attendance.

While attending these meetings, I was introduced to the *Twelve Questions of Marijuana Anonymous*.

Even while sitting in the meetings, listening to other members share their stories, and identifying with their shares, I still questioned whether I was really a marijuana addict.

However, in honestly answering those twelve questions, I became thoroughly convinced that I was indeed a marijuana addict.

### *1. Has using marijuana stopped being fun?*

*Yes.* Using marijuana stopped being fun long before I stopped using it. I felt hopelessness, fear, and a mild paranoia that someone would find out. My days of parties and laughter with marijuana were over. I lived the life of a chameleon, always putting on a changing façade to fit the crowd.

### *2. Do you ever get high alone?*

I often got high alone. I bought two baggies of weed from the dealer—one for my husband and me and another just for me. If *our* bag ran out before we could buy more, I would tell him I had a little stashed away, but more often, I would not.

### 3. Is it hard for you to imagine a life without marijuana?

When I first got clean, it was very hard to imagine life without marijuana. I thought I would become boring, that I would lose my creativity, that the world would lose its color, and that I'd lose my friends. It was certainly hard to stop thinking about it.

### 4. Do you find that your friends are determined by your marijuana use?

I could answer yes to this question, too, being that all my friends were my using buddies. I had a few work friends and a woman who was the mother of my son's friend, but all my *real* friends definitely had to smoke weed. I also never mixed groups of friends. One of my first birthday parties in sobriety included people from all areas of my life except my using buddies. Today all my friends are determined by the quality of their lives and their choices, and I met most of them in recovery.

### 5. Do you smoke marijuana to avoid dealing with your problems or to cope with your feelings?

I'll be honest. While smoking weed, I could not see that I was avoiding problems or feelings. It never occurred to me that I was evading or coping. I smoked weed because I liked how I felt when I was high, and I didn't like how I felt when I wasn't high. After a few months in sobriety, though, I could see many areas where I was definitely avoiding all the problems and feelings as best as I could.

### 6. Has your marijuana use led to financial difficulties and/or legal consequences?

I was arrested, so *yes,* to the legal consequences. Yes, to financial difficulties as well. Though at the time, I didn't connect my use with my financial issues. We had many late payment notices and threats of having our power and telephone shut off; we never saved for the future and once filed for bankruptcy. I had grand dreams and no means to achieve them. After I started the court program, I wondered how I would pay all the legal fees—and I was surprised that not buying weed every week made money start flowing. I did the arithmetic and calculated that I spent about $4,000 a year on marijuana; money I could have saved or spent on other, more important, things,

### 7. Does your marijuana use let you live in a privately defined world?

My personal, privately defined world meant that the rules for everyone else did not apply to me. Once, for instance, I smoked a joint while sitting on a bench waiting for the bus. My friend, who also smoked weed, was surprised. My attitude was that if someone came up to us, I'd just ditch the joint in the weeds and that my friend should chill out.

Another time, my second husband and I smoked a couple of joints on the way to a nice restaurant in an area where parking was scarce. I pulled up to the valet parking—*which I could not really afford*—and handed the keys to the valet, smoke drifting out of the minivan. My husband was shocked and a bit perturbed. I honestly did not understand at the time why he was upset with my behavior.

**8. Have you ever failed to keep promises you made about cutting down or controlling your use of marijuana?**

During that last year, I made many promises to myself and others, only to break those promises time and time again until my promises were a joke. It took a couple of years of staying clean and sober before I earned back the trust of others.

**9. Has your use of marijuana caused problems with health, memory, concentration, or motivation?**

Health-wise, the first thing I remember being concerned about was coughing up tar-like phlegm. I'd cough several times and spit black wads from my throat into the sink. I mentioned it to my husband, who blamed it on the Southern California air we breathed. I thought that was ridiculous, that it might really be the quantities of marijuana I was smoking. I tried a few experiments with tissue paper, the kind you blow your nose into—I'd smoke weed and blow the smoke out through the tissue. A dark yellow-brown stain appeared. Every time. I did this a few times, thinking, "That's going into my lungs." It didn't stop me, but it slowed me down for a week or two.

Memory? Yes, my memory was affected. I attribute memory loss to nothing else. I was young, and I once could remember entire sixteen-digit numbers without a problem. Toward the end of my using, I couldn't remember a single digit long enough to put it in a spreadsheet without double-checking it. I remember looking back and forth, again and again, trying to remember one damn number.

I will say that my ability to remember and recall numbers and other information began to return when I'd been sober for around five years. I remember being excited and relieved. On the flip side, I also remember watching a video of my grandmother's eightieth birthday celebration and seeing myself walk across the screen but not remembering, to this day, attending that event. I remembered the dress I wore in that video, but not my presence.

Concentration and motivation were also affected by my marijuana use. I had difficulty following through with simple assignments, and I was a mediocre employee—though I thought I was the best. I was not motivated to strive for more in my life. For example, I started college in 1991, changed my major four or five times, and received my Associate's Degree in 2016. I could lie and tell you that life was happening—kids, job, and all that—but the truth is this, I didn't care enough for long enough, so it took forever to complete that degree. I was fifty years old, clean and sober thirteen years when I received my college degree and walked with my graduating class.

**10. When your stash is nearly empty, do you feel anxious or worried about how to get more?**

I may have mentioned this... I bought extra bags of marijuana so I wouldn't run out. Sometimes we had to wait days for more weed if our dealer ran out. I absolutely felt anxious and became irritable when that stash ran low. I remember negotiating with my husband about who would make the drive on a weeknight, after dinner—sometimes before dinner—to pick up the weed so we wouldn't be without our precious marijuana for a minute.

**11. Do you plan your life around your marijuana use?**

I did. I made sure I had a plan to leave any event early where I couldn't smoke. I was thinking about my next high while hanging out with friends or family. I canceled events I planned to attend if I was too high, making up reasons—usually my health—about why I had to cancel. I never smoked marijuana before attending a family gathering, and only lasted for a couple of hours before I had to make excuses to leave so I could get high.

**12. Have friends or relatives ever complained that your using is damaging your relationship with them?**

I have to tell you, for a few years, I'd listen to these questions read in meetings, and I always felt proud that this last question was the one I could answer with a resounding *no*.

One day in 2014, while going through boxes of my children's old schoolwork, I came across a letter my oldest son had written to me when he was about fourteen or fifteen, written during the time I was smoking weed with my teenagers. In the letter, he admitted that his position was hypocritical but that he found my behavior "pathetic." Those were the two things I always remember about reading that letter—his courage and my shame. Deep shame. He was the only one who ever "complained," and he did it once, in that letter. I must have read it when I first received it but didn't recall it, even as I read it again. I know today that I caused significant damage to all my relationships, and I had to discover that on my own.

Revisiting the past to answer those questions is painful. I am glad, though, that I don't operate in those ways anymore. I hope that if you have a problem with marijuana, and if you answered those questions for yourself, honestly, you have a better idea of the answer to the question of being a marijuana addict, any sort of addict, or an alcoholic.

If you are still unsure if you have a problem with using marijuana or other substances, I have one more suggestion, which I tried, although I didn't know I was experimenting at the time.

# CHAPTER SEVEN

# An Experiment

I used to think I could quit anytime I wanted to, that I didn't have a problem with weed.

I thought I could quit—that it was still my choice to smoke or not smoke—until I started feeling miserable whenever I used marijuana and made an honest effort to stop smoking. As mentioned previously, I was arrested for felony cultivation and had a prison sentence hanging over my head.

From the date of my arrest, I managed to stay clean from marijuana for fifty-three days—*I counted every single day*—with fear being the great motivator. I suffered through the physical detoxifying of my body. I thought about smoking marijuana all day, every day and was obsessed, but I didn't want to give the judge any reason to carry out the sentence. However, even though I attended twelve-step meetings, I did nothing else. No sponsor meant I had no program to follow, learned no coping skills for sober living, and had no support to lean on. My only motivation was fear. As time passed, that fear faded, and I decided I could just smoke one joint, take one hit, and I could stop after that. After all, I'd stopped smoking for fifty-three days. Instead, I smoked non-stop for three days, and when a new court date inevitably approached, the fear returned, and I white-knuckled it again.

This return to marijuana was repeated twice. At seventy-three days clean, I experienced emotional turmoil following the seeming disappearance of my daughter. She used substances much like I did, without care or discernment. I often felt intense anxiety and hopelessness about her drug use. Whenever I saw a young, dark-haired woman sitting on a curb near a police car flashing its party lights, I'd slow my vehicle as I drove by, hoping that woman wasn't my daughter. I lived in constant fear that one day the sheriff would knock on my door and ask me to come to the coroner's office to identify a body.

When she didn't answer her phone or return messages after several days, my nerves hit their limit, and I couldn't—*wouldn't*—sit with those feelings anymore. Drinking a twelve-pack of beer one Sunday afternoon led to smoking marijuana.

On June 6, 2003, I stopped drinking alcohol, recognizing if I drank alcohol, I'd eventually smoke again. I was clear-headed enough to make that connection about myself.

My last run with marijuana was in October 2003, with ninety-three days clean. My second husband and I took a road trip to visit the two children who'd left our dysfunctional home to live with their mother in another state. We were going to celebrate Halloween. We took my youngest son and my daughter with us, a little family reunion. I started smoking on the sly the minute we hit the first rest stop and didn't stop until we returned home. We spent about three days before Halloween visiting with family, getting high whenever we could.

On the afternoon of Halloween, I had my moment of clarity—a lightning bolt of insight. Actively reasoning out which relative to drop off my youngest son with so I could get high, I heard a strong, clear voice between my ears boom, "What the *fuck* do you think you're doing?" I swerved the vehicle a little; the volume of that voice startled me that much.

## An Experiment

I was immediately aware of and embarrassed by my behavior. I'd love to tell you that I stopped right then and there, but I still had some weed left to smoke. I quit three days later, for good, and decided to look for a guide or mentor—a sponsor—in those meetings I attended.

If you aren't sure if you are an addict, I propose an experiment as a birds-eye view of your behavior when you aren't using marijuana. *Disclaimer*: I didn't do this, but I know long-time members who've suggested this technique to newer members—members who repeatedly stated that maybe they were wrong, maybe they weren't an addict or alcoholic.

One technique is controlled using—only smoking after work, just on Saturdays, or only twice a day. If you find that you have trouble sticking to your controlled using, you may have a problem.

The technique I propose is to select a date to temporarily stop using marijuana for fifteen days. Utilizing a simple wall calendar, record physical feelings, emotions like depression, sadness, anger, rage, irritability, and impatience, and experiences, like saying "sorry" often or swearing more than usual. It might be a good idea to also record recurring thoughts. For instance, I constantly daydreamed about what the day after I received my one-year chip would look like because I was only going to be clean for that year.

When those fifteen days are up, review the results—the things you wrote on the calendar. After reviewing the feelings, emotions, and experiences recorded on the calendar, ask yourself again, "Am I a marijuana addict?" Decide if you think you have a problem with using marijuana.

During that process of gathering sober days then using again, then gathering more days before using again, I had this valuable insight; each time I quit lasted longer than the time before.

A friend in this program knew she had a problem with pot. She attended meetings, and she wasn't ready to quit. She'd smoke all week and showed up for several consecutive weekly meetings. She eventually opted to share at a particular meeting, so one day chose not to smoke because anyone sharing at that meeting was asked to go twenty-four hours without substance use. Her first share was about coming to the meeting each week, then smoking in the car before she headed home. Every week after her first share, she stayed clean on Friday and smoked less and less during the week. Eventually, she chose to stop smoking altogether. That's what it took for her, and no one else made that choice for her.

This is a difficult transition, honestly making this admission to yourself. A sentence in the book *Alcoholics Anonymous* reads, "No person likes to think he is bodily and mentally different from his fellows." I certainly didn't. I spent most of my life, well into sobriety, being who I thought others wanted me to be so I could fit in and feel accepted.

We all wish to be a part of something, not just to fit in but to belong, to be accepted. In my case, I wanted to belong to a group where I could be accepted as myself, even as I discovered who that was. It took some time before I admitted to myself that I could not smoke weed every once in a while or manage my life well when I did. It took me a while longer to find a group where I felt like I belonged.

# CHAPTER EIGHT

## We Don't Want You Here

An unusual limbo exists for a marijuana addict. It results from others' perceptions that marijuana is not addictive. I, too, believed that marijuana was harmless, and it did not occur to me that my using hurt anyone else. I certainly didn't think it was addictive. And I still hear several times a year—from newcomers and healthcare professionals—that they had never heard about Marijuana Anonymous.

I have one variation of an addictive personality, meaning I'm more likely to become addicted to something, whether behavior or substance. I tend to overuse something to distract me from my feelings when I become uncomfortable with those feelings. This is a very general statement, as the concept of an addictive personality is multifaceted and looks different from personality to personality. Let's just say that distraction easily helps me avoid my feelings, and it takes a great deal of effort and practice to sit with my feelings and experience them. The jury is still out on whether I was born this way, trained, or a little bit of both. Regardless, a preference for distraction is a part of me.

For generations, addiction and alcoholism have run high in my family on both sides of the family tree. I was introduced to twelve-step programs through a close family member in my twenties. I probably attended half a dozen or so meetings with that member, showing up as an invited guest to witness the acceptance of anniversary cakes and hear shares about the struggle, the solution, and the message. I was no stranger to the rooms. Yet, when standing before the judge requesting the PC 1000 drug diversion program, I completely forgot that there was a recovery program for marijuana addiction. Even though I'd attended a handful of meetings, I was a little fuzzy on the whole twelve-step program concept. The court bailiff gave me a list of resources and a requirement to have a proof of attendance card signed weekly at a twelve-step meeting. Nowhere on that list was a phone number for a marijuana addict support group.

Since I was required to attend meetings, I went to the group I'd had the most exposure to in my family. My first recovery meeting was an in-person meeting of Alcoholics Anonymous or A.A. I hadn't yet decided if I was an alcoholic—*I am*—and I hadn't yet learned the vital lesson of looking for the similarities when people spoke rather than the differences I heard. I listened to the other members share their stories in that first in-person meeting, and I thought, *Oh my God, these people are messed up! How can anyone drink leftover, warm vodka first thing in the morning before they even get out of bed?* I took a chance and shared in that meeting about my marijuana problem, and after the meeting, a member kindly told me, "We only discuss alcoholism in this room." I decided that those meetings were not for me.

The second in-person meeting I attended was with Narcotics Anonymous, or N.A. for short. At the beginning of twelve-step meetings, the members go around the room introducing themselves and saying they are an addict or an alcoholic. When it was my turn, I said my name and that I was a marijuana addict. Many of the other members laughed or shook their heads, and I distinctly heard, "Come back when you have a real disease." I immediately felt small, uncomfortable, and unwelcome. I scratched that group off my list.

Limbo is defined as an indeterminate state. According to the law, marijuana was illegal. I was charged with a felony for growing it. And the courts treated marijuana like a drug problem, but anonymous programs thought marijuana addiction was a sham, a "wanna-be" addiction. I felt lost. Where was I going to find a group that didn't think my addiction was weak, minor, or fake?

The next time I attended the drug diversion class, I read all the papers posted on the bulletin board while waiting my turn to pee in a cup to prove I hadn't been smoking. The board was covered with meeting lists, phone lists, and other recovery-related items. On that day, right in the middle of the board was a half-sheet flyer with those little tear-off strips on the bottom containing a phone number.

This question was printed on the flyer in big block letters: *Has smoking pot stopped being fun?*

Eureka! I tore off a strip and later called to find a meeting. I discovered a meeting five minutes from my office on Thursday nights. The following Thursday I attended, and by the time I left that meeting, I knew I'd found my people. They smoked like I smoked; they lied like I lied, and they wanted to quit. Together they were learning how to live life without marijuana. They also had a book that might offer a solution. I was in.

Another member came into the program the same way I did, through the court system. The judge gave him that same list of recovery resources, and he called the number for A.A. He explained to the person on the other end of the line that he needed to attend meetings and get a card signed. The A.A. person asked my friend how much alcohol he drank, and my friend replied that he smoked marijuana. The A.A. person paused and then replied, "Well, we don't want you here." Rude. Fortunately, the A.A. person gave him the number for Marijuana Anonymous, so that's progress. But, still, that's the attitude I also experienced, "We don't want you here."

I've heard similar stories from new members who come to the marijuana meetings from rehabilitation centers and recovery homes. As marijuana users, our addiction is not taken as seriously as addictions to other drugs or alcohol. Members of other recovery groups tell us with certainty that marijuana isn't an addictive substance.

This type of thinking keeps a lot of marijuana addicts out of recovery, trying to figure out for themselves how to get clean and stay that way. I remember being surprised to learn that I could have gotten some help in a rehabilitation facility. Discovering that people attended rehab for marijuana addiction helped me to share that experience with others and to let them know not to take the attitude of other addicts or alcoholics personally.

I know that, for me, marijuana was a problem. Marijuana use distorted my worldview, while I believed that my perspective was not distorted. As previously stated, marijuana puts us in circles with people who provide access to all the other drugs we use.

On a monthly, sometimes weekly basis, I hear the words below in the rooms of recovery:

"I'd never heard of Marijuana Anonymous before today."

"I've been going to A. A. for a while now because I didn't know there was a program for marijuana addicts."

"I never would have guessed marijuana was something I could be addicted to."

I can absolutely relate.

I attend both marijuana and alcohol recovery meetings, as I qualify for both programs. I keep an open mind, and I attend both to stay clean and sober.

Once, an A.A. friend asked me why I attended both programs, not just A.A. My response was that my early experiences showed me I am more accepted in the rooms of M.A., that marijuana addicts seemed to be more open-minded and accepting, and that attracted me to recovery. Alcoholics Anonymous is where the twelve-step movement began, and I am forever grateful to God, Bill W., and Dr. Bob. Marijuana Anonymous, however, is my home.

This was my first experience with *willingness*. I was willing to submit to this program to stay out of jail and keep a felony off my record. Willingness was my gift from desperation. This was the beginning of my life of sobriety and recovery.

I am a marijuana addict. That's the substance I used the most and the longest, and that's the last substance I quit using. For me, the solution for staying clean and sober became clear while attending twelve-step recovery support meetings. Once I got sober, I embarked on the journey of recovery.

## CHAPTER NINE

# From Sobriety to Recovery

*I* used to think that sobriety and recovery were the same thing, interchangeable, but now I know the difference.

I learned, eventually, that sobriety is abstinence—not using the substance anymore, whatever that substance might be: marijuana, alcohol, methamphetamines, cocaine, heroin, sex, etcetera. I learned that sobriety would only take me so far. I mentioned earlier that I had a series of days when I didn't use. I also didn't have a plan in place when I felt inclined to pick up my substance of choice—marijuana—again. I didn't think ahead to what I'd do after I stopped using.

Abstaining–stopping the use—is a temporary fix. All my coping behaviors were still in play. Once I had stopped using for a while, I became intolerable and cranky, irritated and frustrated, prickly. I wanted to change those feelings, and using marijuana was the only solution I knew up to that point.

I discovered my problem while attending meetings and reading recovery literature; I didn't know how to live life sober. I was still doing the same old things sober that I'd been doing loaded—lying to myself, manipulating others, intimidating others, justifying my behaviors, and blaming other people for my current situation.

I got high to do everything. Some people get high to celebrate, relax, or take the edge off. I also got high to get ready for work, grocery shop, take a walk, write a report, or do my job. A friend once said, "If I'm breathing, I'm smoking," and I could relate.

Beyond sobriety or abstinence is recovery. Recovery is a process where I recover from the things that sent me into the void in the first place. Marijuana use was just a visible symptom of a bigger issue I didn't even acknowledge—denial of pain I've carried for years. The same goes for drinking too much. When I spent a few days drunk, I'd disconnect from my physical and emotional feelings. I had no idea why I behaved or responded the way I did, and I avoided sitting in stillness long enough to figure it out.

In working a recovery program—reading literature, answering questions about my history, and listening to others share similar stories—I discovered where I came from, why I first turned to marijuana, and why I used it for so long. I was given an opportunity to learn to identify those behaviors and habits that no longer served me. I learned to recognize my behaviors and choose if I wanted to continue practicing those behaviors and habits. Over time, I slowly learned different ways to deal with the same issues, issues that cropped up again and again until I faced them head-on.

Another essential component to this formula I've heard shared in meetings many times over the years is determining if you're getting sober and practicing recovery for yourself or because of someone else.

Spoiler alert: the only person I can get sober for is *me*. Many come to meetings to get the law, the spouse, the employer, their friends, their parents, or even their kids off their backs. I have not yet heard a success story that stems from doing the work for someone else. The addict must be their own reason *why*.

We each have an a-ha moment when we realize that we must do this sobriety and recovery thing for ourselves.

My *why* way back then went something like this. When I got arrested for felony cultivation, I believed even then that I'd been arrested because of the choices I'd made in my life up to that point. I believed that I was being offered an opportunity that I didn't even understand yet to make a change, a change in my attitudes and my behaviors.

When I started attending meetings, a court requirement, I met people who had smoked weed the same way I did, all day, every day. They shared that they never planned to stop using cannabis. Then their lives got messy. And there they were, clean and sober, learning a program that provided tools to help them live life sober, one day at a time.

I was happy for them, and I liked hearing what they had to say, and I could relate to their shares. Still, I planned to hang out just long enough to learn how to smoke in a controlled fashion and get that one-year chip to show myself and those others that I could quit. I attended these meetings to appease the court system and stay out of jail.

Something happened during that first year, though, something quite unexpected. I realized that I had a problem with living, that I had been avoiding my feelings and allowing others to call the shots most of my life, and as a result, I smoked weed to hide my weakness and cowardice from myself. When I began to change my thinking, I saw light, hope, and a way of life I could become comfortable in. I found that if I chose to continue to know myself better, I might become a whole individual, practicing consistent behaviors, feeling comfortable in my own skin, and even comfortable while feeling uncomfortable.

I chose to work the twelve-step program as suggested, with a sponsor, for myself. No one else was important enough to me, and I was slowly becoming important to myself. Very slowly, but it was happening.

My internal shift happened one day as I was driving to work. I was thinking about all the things I heard in the meetings and read in the literature. What I was learning about myself and my thinking was changing minutely. I realized that if I continued down this path and embraced this new way of thinking and behaving, everything I was connected to would change, too, like a ripple.

I asked myself if I was willing to continue growing into this new version of me, knowing that things around me might change. Was I ready to continue down this recovery path, knowing I might change? Who was I doing this for? Me or someone else? And I knew the answer right away. If I wanted to stay sober and recover from all that was done to me and all I'd done to myself, I would continue on this path. Period. I was six months sober.

I got that one-year chip, and instead of returning to the life of a marijuana user, I continued to stay sober, and I reluctantly worked the steps with my sponsor. I say reluctantly because I dragged my feet. Yeah, I wanted sobriety, but the recovery part–digging up all my hurts and resentments—scared me. The person I was when I walked into those recovery rooms is not the same person I am today. Every day, if I do the work, I change for the better. I am a better version of myself when I put a recovery program before anything else in my life. When I'm working the steps daily, putting my faith in a power greater than myself, and just doing the next right thing, I attract good things in my life.

What kinds of good things do I attract? Well, first, I can be myself with anybody. I no longer have to pretend or be a chameleon, changing my personality to match the likes or dislikes of whoever I am with at the moment, friend or lover. Another thing I attract is people who want a real connection, people who feel their feelings, avoid gossip, and walk away from drama. We talk about spirit, emotion, challenges, and how we apply the principles we've learned to our lives. We also laugh a lot, and sometimes we cry. I have fewer friends than I did when I was using, but I have truer friends, too.

I am comfortable in my own skin most of the time. I can also walk through life feeling uncomfortable without needing to run from those feelings. I am recovering from my childhood, my adulthood, and my addiction. I see how much my attitude towards life and people has changed so far in practicing this program of recovery.

There is plenty of joy in sobriety today, a multitude of reasons to feel happiness. Getting sober and continuing to work that program of recovery was a generator of many joyful moments in those first twelve months.

Slowly rebuilding a life worth living, I look back on a handful of wonderful memories I created.

Just after celebrating six years of sobriety, my second husband and I flew to South Korea to meet our new grandson, born to my son and his wife, on a U.S. Army base. International flights, passports, car rentals—the works. Like grown-ups.

Two years later, we drove from California to Lubbock, Texas, to meet our hours-old granddaughter and spent a week getting to know her. Three years after that, in 2014, I was again granted the privilege of meeting the next granddaughter and spending a week with both her and her sister.

I was invited. I was present. I remember many of the little moments spent with these new people in my life, my grandchildren. My children wanted me to be present, to share in their delight, with their growing families.

Other blessings—gifts really—included simple things, like a registered, insured vehicle and a current driver's license. No longer concerned about being pulled over, worried that the police would detain me for driving under the influence, I felt pride when saying I was returning from a recovery meeting.

Financially, I am a trustworthy member of society. Banks allow me to take out loans for cars and houses. I have credit cards I manage responsibly, honoring the agreement to pay back that which I've borrowed.

One of my biggest markers of personal growth is the kind of partner I am in my romantic relationship. Following the divorce from my second husband, I swore I'd never marry again. There were many sound reasons for this promise to myself. However, I found myself in a relationship several months after my separation from my second husband. Long story short, two years later, I married once more. There were differences this last time, however. I'd been sober for over ten years, working a recovery program, working on myself. My new husband was clean and sober, too. I wasn't pregnant. I made a conscious, intentional choice to spend my life with this man. The first several years weren't always easy. Life showed us what we were made of and what we could be if we learned from our differences, grew together in love. And I work at communicating better, being open-minded, compromising, and practicing love and forgiveness. I maintain my identity—the one I've cultivated since I started sobriety and recovery—while working to be a good partner to my friend and husband.

The biggest take-away I can offer is my attitude and how it's changed over the years. I look for the good in every situation. I remember that change is the only constant and that the good times pass just like the bad times do. I can carry around a sour attitude and share it with others, or I can bring my A-game, my smile and my patience, accepting what is and hoping my attitude of gratitude is contagious.

Life still has its challenges, but how I choose to respond is still the only power I have that remains consistent.

What am I trying to share in this chapter? For me, recovery means *me* recovering from all the habits and behaviors—all the coping mechanisms—I developed growing up. It also means healing in a deep and foundational way so that as I move forward in life, I leave an uplifting ripple behind me and all around me that brings a feeling of pride.

If you decide to embark on a path of addiction recovery, do it for you. That's all. My recovery benefits every single person I encounter—family, friends, employers, employees, teammates, and even total strangers. Our behaviors got us here, to this place of discontent prisoner of a substance. We must change our thoughts and behaviors if we want our life to change. It really is as simple as that.

I had to ask myself, *Am I happy with the way my life is unfolding right now?* The answer was *no*, and I had to consider that marijuana use was the reason.

I didn't have to do anything I didn't want to do. I could quit going to meetings at any time. But everything I'd seen and heard appealed to me, and the life I lived before I started going to meetings no longer did. I chose to continue sobriety and take the recovery program seriously.

In the next section, I'll share what many long-timers know that helped me to turn sober days into sober years.

## PART TWO

# After I Quit Smoking Weed

The words on the flyer asked, "Has smoking pot stopped being fun?" And for me, it had.

When I stopped smoking marijuana, it was still illegal in California. I've never vaped, dabbed, or had edibles. The potency of marijuana has increased since I stopped smoking. From what I hear in shares by newcomers, the potency of 2003 was child's play compared to the stuff people buy in dispensaries now. A friend of mine, a former smoker, purchased some dispensary weed for a medical condition. He told me that one toke left him useless for hours. He couldn't process a thought, staring at the television with zero comprehension. Time passed, and he missed it.

I don't know what it's like to get high in 2022. I have heard users speak of cannabinoid hyperemesis syndrome (CHS), which sounds horrible. The Cedars-Sinai website describes it as "a condition that leads to repeated and severe bouts of vomiting. It is rare and only occurs in daily long-term users of marijuana."

Having attended three online meetings a week since the COVID-19 pandemic struck, I've learned that CHS is no longer as rare as it once was. Although I did not experience it, I've heard from many marijuana users who have. Marijuana didn't make me nauseous; it took away my nausea, much like it does for people who require chemotherapy. I want to include a nod to the dangers of CHS here because it is a thing among chronic marijuana users, and age is not a factor.

It is difficult to explain to non-addictive persons what it is like to be a marijuana addict, drug addict, or alcoholic. If you've gotten this far, though, you know that I've tried.

Nor can I explain what recovery is like for me, on my journey, to someone who hasn't traveled down this portion of the path. I'll spend the next several chapters relaying my story of what early recovery was like for me.

I now understand what faith feels like and the purpose of finding a higher power that works for me, but it took me years before faith and higher power made sense.

I learned how to trust, too, but—again—I came to understand what trust looked like first and that I had to trust myself before I could extend trust to others.

I spent a lot of time in early recovery doing the bare minimum to stay sober and pretending that I understood what was going on in those recovery rooms when, in truth, I didn't have a clue. It took me a long time to admit I didn't understand what was being said and to ask someone to explain things clearly to me in a way that made sense.

Even when I began understanding how the program worked, I did not follow the suggestions. I thought I could find an easier, softer way. When I was very new to the program, I would tweak the instructions for the steps, attempting to "fix" the program and make it more palatable to my taste instead of giving someone else's experience a chance.

If you are even a little bit like me, it might have taken a while to admit that you have a problem with marijuana or other substances. It may have come as a surprise to you that you don't have all the answers and need to ask for help. And if you are a *lot* like me, pretending that you understand what people are saying—nodding and smiling—when you don't is second nature, an old behavior.

My entire life is filled with examples of me learning lessons the hard way, through trial and error, and more trials until I finally figured it out. I wasn't someone who asked for help, and it took me years to learn that the easier, softer way was in a community of others, asking for assistance when I got stuck and that it was okay for me to utilize that community. Asking for help is not a weakness; I just didn't know that for a long time.

Staying sober and living a life of recovery is simple, they say, but not easy. Recovery is the healing portion of sobriety, the part where I learn how to stay sober, no matter what.

In the following chapters, I share my experience during my early sobriety that affected the quality of my recovery. Attempt these simple actions consistently and experience quality recovery more quickly.

# CHAPTER TEN

# Detoxification

After I chose sobriety, I experienced a detoxification period, the process of flushing all the toxins and impurities out of the body. And much like quitting cigarettes or sugar, there is a period of adjustment. Several symptoms may show up when a person quits smoking marijuana, including nausea, insomnia, irritability, depression, anxiety, emotional outbursts, zero motivation, mind fog, cravings, obsession, vivid dreams, weight loss or gain, and the potential for cross-addiction.

I experienced all of them. Other recovering marijuana addicts experienced none, some or all, when they stopped using marijuana, too. Having lived through the initial detox is one of the reasons I've never picked up again—I never want to have to go through detoxification again.

I had no idea there would be any ill effects from quitting marijuana. I used to think marijuana didn't affect me, and I discovered that pot might be slowly poisoning me.

Nausea was the first symptom I experienced each time I quit. Nausea became unbearable after a day or two, so I smoked marijuana to relieve it. After several of those cycles, it occurred to me that *not* smoking marijuana might be the reason for nausea, and the next time I quit smoking pot, I toughed it out. Much like getting over the stomach flu, the nausea passed after a couple of days. I ate a lot of unsalted soda crackers and drank a lot of water.

Broken sleep, or insomnia, is normal at the beginning of sobriety; cannabis helped me sleep. My first solution to insomnia was falling asleep to lighthearted movies. *Ice Age, Monsters, Inc., The Fifth Element,* and *Galaxy Quest* put me to sleep every night during that first year. If I woke up in the middle of the night, which happened often, I'd whisper the Serenity Prayer over and over to drown out all the thoughts competing for attention in my head. I took naps on the weekends. Sometimes I even slept on the couch as a courtesy to my spouse. Morning caffeine intake increased for a while, too.

Depression and anxiety no longer hid behind a veil of smoke. Depression was a low, heavy feeling, more than sadness, and was accompanied by a lack of motivation. I found it difficult to get out of bed each morning. Tasks like getting my child ready for school or myself ready for work were huge challenges. Some days I pushed through, and other days I called in sick. It took me a while to recognize a pattern. Depression ebbed and flowed. I wanted to live a productive life, so I learned and developed techniques to help me live with depression. Knowing how to manage it when it came and knowing it was temporary helped me accept it.

In 2018, when I was fifteen years sober, I was professionally diagnosed with chronic mild depression, which means that my brain doesn't always produce the proper balance of chemicals and hormones. I also learned that many people in recovery have chemical imbalances in the brain. Some have the mild but consistent depression I experience, while others have deeper depression, bipolar disorder, or schizoaffective disorder, to name a few.

When I wake up and recognize that low feeling, I acknowledge that the day will be more challenging. I have a daily morning routine, and I start with the first item on the list, while accepting how I feel emotionally and physically. Sometimes I feel weepy and sad, so I share that with my spouse, and I reach out to my sponsor or other friends. It isn't the way I'd like things to be, but this is the way it is sometimes.

Acceptance of how things are, instead of how I'd like things to be, is a lesson that's taken me years to learn, and acceptance provides a level of serenity that helps me through life's hard times.

Eventually, the depressive feeling passes, sometimes that morning, and more usually over about three or four days. What I don't do is let the depression paralyze me—I keep moving, albeit more slowly. I remember that this feeling will pass, and it will also return. It's a part of me, of who I am, and I can navigate through it using the techniques I've learned and practiced. Sometimes I choose to stay in bed or return to bed and stream movies that make me laugh.

Anxiety is another symptom I began to notice once I stopped smoking weed. I had no idea that marijuana was making an existing condition—fear about social situations—manageable because I'd never been clean long enough to feel the full effects of anxiety. I often experience anxiety before attending an event. For example, I may be really excited about attending a group gathering up until the day of the event. On event day, I may spend a few hours talking myself into going. I used to talk myself out of going to events a lot; instead, I'd stay home and get high.

I usually talk myself through the fear by identifying where the anxiety originated. Calling a friend and sharing how I feel lessens the feeling of fear. I find that if I follow through with attending those seemingly scary social gatherings, when it's all over, I'm glad I went, and I often have a good time while I'm there. The anxiety usually melts away within the first ten minutes. In the end, though, I do what I am capable of doing to take care of me.

I also experience anxiety when I overdo outside stimulation, when I try to accomplish more than I allowed time to complete. My previous solution to anxiety was to smoke some weed to mellow out. I have learned new, healthier techniques for coping with anxiety that replace smoking weed.

If I have a busy day, by the afternoon, my stress level increases and I become short-tempered and snippy. Stepping away, taking a break, and practicing breathing exercises help calm me down. Withdrawing from people for a short period also helps. I review the tasks I think I need to complete and decide which are most important. Picking the top two or three to complete, I let the rest go for another day.

Yeah, sometimes life is more uncomfortable for a longer period, but today I'm in charge of my feelings and responses instead of avoiding them.

Each of the conditions mentioned above has an emotional aspect, and at the beginning of sobriety, my emotions were all over the place. At the time I chose to get sober, I was familiar with a few emotions—anger, sadness, and happiness. During the detox, unfamiliar emotions came and went at will, which was hard on me, and all my family members. Over time I learned to recognize and deal with my emotions. I discovered that there are many nuances to those few emotions that I knew.

My responses were often pouty and childish. Maybe you can relate. Most situations brought me to anger quickly, usually because I wasn't getting my way. During those first few months attending recovery meetings, I found it difficult to sit still, and every small noise annoyed me—people shuffling their chairs, fiddling with their keys, or getting up to go to the bathroom. People laughing during the meeting was a huge irritation. *What the hell are they laughing about anyway*, I thought. *This sobriety was serious life or death business!* I felt edgy a lot of the time.

The term "mind fog" was not one I knew, but I experienced this, too. I found it difficult to keep my thoughts straight. I forgot things easily. I couldn't remember what I was doing from one room to the next. I started setting alarms on my phone to avoid missing appointments and meetings.

Thinking about weed all the time is an example of an obsession of the mind. Since I previously smoked from sunup to sundown, I still thought about weed from sunup to sundown even though I stopped using it. When I was idle, some of the members of the committee in my head worked hard to make a case for smoking just a little bit. To distract myself from those thoughts, I got busy filling every hour with activity.

Right before bedtime was the hardest time for me, and Friday through Sunday were the longest days early on; my cravings were strong. Once I ran out of activities at home, I had to get creative. I read more, visited parks with the kids, and attended extra meetings. I grew tomatoes and other vegetables.

Dreams, which had been absent for years, became constant and vivid. I had many using dreams as well, waking up in a panic, convinced I had blown all those days I'd accumulated, then becoming angry and relieved at the same time when I realized it was only a dream. The feelings of failure and guilt that came with some of those emotional dreams lingered for a day or two sometimes.

I don't know if today's cannabis or edibles trigger the munchies, but I certainly wanted to snack when I was getting high. In sobriety, I lost some weight in the beginning. I wasn't eating nearly as much food, and I was moving all the time now, running from that obsessive craving with all the activity. Others share about replacing pot with food and gaining weight.

Each of these symptoms happens with each of us to varying degrees when we quit. It's different for everyone, but I hope that knowing what you might experience during your first several weeks will help arm you with a defense plan to deal with whatever arises for you.

## CHAPTER ELEVEN

# Who Am I Recovering For?

"Oh, I know."
I said that a lot, and I usually didn't know. There was so much I pretended to know. I was afraid I wouldn't fit in if I admitted that I didn't know something.

Ask anyone who's spent a little time in an addiction recovery program. No one comes into the rooms of recovery on a good day. I haven't met a person yet who woke up one day thinking, *When I grow up, I want to be a drug addict or an alcoholic.*

I don't know when I crossed the line from wanting to smoke marijuana to *having* to smoke marijuana, but I do know that it took me years to realize I was an addict, and while I hoped it would be easy, it was unrealistic of me to think that getting sober was going to make everything in my life better overnight. If you are reading this, maybe you, too, hoped for a quick, three-step plan to quit using and "become normal" again.

Sorry. Recovery takes work. The best three-part plan, essential for success, I can suggest is living by these words—honesty, open mind, and willingness. That's H.O.W. most of us got sober and stayed that way, despite life happening.

## Honesty

Honesty has many levels. There is cash register honesty, as in, I realized that the cashier gave me too much change and I returned the difference, or I left the store with an item tucked under my arm, and I return to the store to pay for it or give it back.

There's honesty with others when I stop lying about everything, like why I was late or where some of the petty cash went.

And finally, honesty with ourselves about who we really are, how we really feel most of the time, and that all our behaviors and habits are less than stellar. This last one, honesty with self, is the most difficult and takes the most time to restore.

## Open Mind

In the book *Alcoholics Anonymous* is a quote by Herbert Spenser at the end of the second appendix, Spiritual Experience, that ends with the words, *". . . contempt prior to investigation."*

An easier way to understand this phrase might be asking, "How do you know you don't like it? You haven't even tried it." An open mind means that before I dismiss a suggestion from someone who has been sober longer than I have, I try it. I spent a lot of time saying *yes* to someone's suggestion—a suggestion that might have saved me a bit of time and suffering—and then *didn't* do the thing they suggested. I still fight that stubborn behavior to this day. When someone suggests an alternative solution to a problem, my first thought is, *I don't need your help. I can figure this out all by myself.* These days, though, my response is usually, "Thanks, I might give that a try."

Having an open mind means admitting to myself that I might not know everything about everything and that I can benefit from someone else's experience.

## Willingness

Right on the heels of having an open mind is willingness. Willingness is when my ego puts down the gloves.

Today I can listen to a suggestion, and I usually take action, but I have moments when I still want to do it my way. When it comes to sobriety and recovery, many people start with being willing to be willing. We aren't saying yes just yet, but we start saying maybe.

Each of us brings baggage when we arrive at the gates of recovery, stuff held onto since early childhood for most of us. It will take time to sort through all that stuff to find the *us* that got lost way back when. It can be done, though; it begins with practicing honesty with self, having an open mind, and the willingness to try something new.

A little help from our friends also goes a long way. When you embark on this journey, you'll find strangers are friends you haven't met yet. In the rooms of recovery, you will meet your tribe.

## CHAPTER TWELVE

# Finding A Tribe

**Tribe**, *noun* trīb\
**Definition of tribe**, from Webster's New World College Dictionary, Fifth Edition
**2:** A group of persons having a common character, occupation, or interest

*I* used to think that I didn't need anyone's help, that I could figure it out on my own, but now I know that I can go farther faster with the help of others. I am a people pleaser, a coping mechanism I learned as a child and honed to perfection. This skill made me a valuable employee, an excellent student, and the friend everyone wanted. I said yes to every assignment, helped classmates with their studies, and did whatever it took to be sure I was liked and included, even if it meant putting myself last—and it usually did. As a result of this behavior, I forgot who I was along the way.

Trust was another casualty of my childhood. As a young person, I experienced betrayal by the people I believed I could count on to love me and watch out for me no matter what. That trust was the hardest thing for me to regain in others and myself.

I once trusted people first, without question, and after repeated betrayals, it became something others had to earn from me. After a while, even that wasn't happening. I built an invisible wall between everyone else and me; I only shared surface stuff. No one was going to get close enough to hurt me again. No one.

The first meetings I attended were online meetings. We "met" in an online chat room set up specifically for marijuana addicts. We could use our names, but I found out later most of the attendees used made-up names. I liked the online chat meetings—complete anonymity since we were all just typing to chat—and I shared honestly because no one knew my identity. I learned much about recovery in that room during my first several months. In those online rooms was the first time I experienced a form of acceptance. After my first relapse, I returned to the chat room. I received support and love instead of rejection, and people kept typing the phrase "keep coming back."

Locating an in-person meeting was more of a challenge, and I put it off for as long as possible.

My first regular in-person marijuana recovery meeting, one I stayed with for a few years, consisted of about five or six people. Every Thursday evening, we met in a church conference room. A comfortable couch, some armchairs and a coffee table furnished the room. Members would sit in a casual circle, read from the book *Life With Hope*, and share about how they related to what was read.

That meeting became my home meeting, as in I'd come home. I learned to feel comfortable being one of many marijuana addicts in recovery. Some of them were like me, genuinely interested in staying sober. They attended the meetings because they wanted to, with a desire to change their behaviors and be there for others, sharing their experience, strength, and hope. It was the first time I felt like I belonged instead of trying to fit in. No one laughed when I said I was a marijuana addict, and I could relate to many of their shares or stories. I consistently attended every Thursday night after work.

I wasn't ready to fully trust them yet—that came later—but I was willing to show up, be respectful, and share as honestly as I could while keeping them at a distance.

When my diversion classes ended, I added a second recovery meeting to my schedule. I had been attending those drug diversion classes—the ones required by the court as a part of the PC 1000 program—on Friday evenings because Friday was when I really got going for the weekend. When the final diversion class approached, I felt fear. I replaced my old habit of heading home to celebrate the end of the week with beer and weed with a new habit that was less destructive, going to those classes. I was afraid of going home after work the following Friday and giving in to the temptation of my old habits, so I found another twelve-step meeting to attend instead.

The new meeting was a candlelight meeting, where actual wax candles burned during the meeting. When the sharing portion of the meeting began, the lights in the room were turned off. With the lights out and the candles burning, everybody was in the shadows. Being in the shadows also made it easier for me to share more openly and honestly.

Attending those meetings, I somehow got it into my head that I had to become friends with everyone in the room. I hugged everyone because other people hugged everyone. I thought, *That's what they do, so that's what I'll do.*

Remember, I am a people pleaser and a chameleon. I was still operating from an old set of rules. As the years passed, I matured and realized I didn't have to hug or even be friends with *everyone* in the room. It was enough that I shared honestly about what I was dealing with each week and how I applied the steps I was learning in real-life situations.

Eventually, I developed a small group of people I trusted who became my tribe. I built a door in my invisible wall and let them in.

The Friday meeting was led a little differently than the Thursday meeting, and I came to learn that every recovery meeting is a little different because the members of each meeting get to decide how their meeting functions.

Generally, each twelve-step meeting I attended started with the Serenity Prayer and introductions. Often readings were handed out before the meeting, and various people read those out loud when asked. A secretary introduced people with meeting commitments, like talking about the literature or handing out milestone chips. Some meetings had a topic picked by the leader, while other meetings read from recovery literature. After the topic was announced or the literature reading concluded, people in the room would share about the topic or the reading and how they related to what they heard and how it applied to their recovery. Some people shared the pain they were going through emotionally during early recovery, and others shared about how they walked through a personal challenge without making things worse. At the end of the meeting, someone led the rest of the group out with a prayer.

I've been attending meetings since 2003, and I get something useful from every meeting I attend.

I feel I should mention that twelve-step meetings are based on a spiritual program. Spirituality—whatever spiritual means to you—is a part of the recovery process. The word God is mentioned in almost every meeting I've ever been in and written in much of the literature. God, for many, is interchangeable with a higher power or a power greater than self. For some members, GOD is an acronym for good orderly direction. I didn't have a problem with the word God or its concept, but many people do. A person can be agnostic or atheist and still be a member of the group, each finding a higher power of their own understanding. Since this book is about my experience, I'll just share about that.

I'll first say that I do not attend a church or belong to any organized religion.

When I was a kid, my parents attended church, and I attended Sunday school. When I was around eight years old, my father joined a new and different church. Something about that organization felt not quite right, and I was glad when we stopped attending that church.

Years later, during my early recovery, a friend invited me to her church. I attended for a while, searching for my idea of a higher power. I enjoyed the pastor's sermons, relating real-life stories using the bible stories as his guide. However, I stopped attending that church due to circumstances that would make another book. I never found a reason to return to any organized religion. I found what I needed for my spiritual journey in the meeting rooms, developing a strong faith in a higher power.

One of the things I found so inviting about the program of recovery was being able to choose my own God, a higher power of *my* understanding. Not yours or his or hers, or any religion's. "*God, as we understood God*" is how the literature reads.

When I chose sobriety, I still believed in God. My belief, a holdover from Sunday school, was an old white man with a long beard who loved me, looked after me, and had my best interests at heart. As an adult, I believed God had given up on me because of my life's choices. I didn't blame God.

What I discovered, though, was that I'd turned my back on the Creator, on that One Spark, on the Universe, on the Divine—whatever you choose to call your higher power—I'd cut myself off from my spiritual guide. I operated on my terms, forcing outcomes I desired instead of letting go of the outcomes. While working on my recovery, it took me six years to find a higher power of my understanding. That relationship with the Universe is much different than when I was a child or a practicing drug addict. I let go of thinking I could control the outcome of anything except for my response to situations, circumstances and people. I have a relationship with my higher power that I don't try to define anymore. It's taken a long time to get to a place where I allow the evolution of my spiritual connection to continue, seeking to improve my conscious contact without trying to explain it.

Each of us in recovery has the opportunity to develop a relationship with our personal higher power, a spiritual connection that works for us and no one else. Whatever that relationship looks like is between each member and their higher power. It takes time to develop that connection, practicing patience and perseverance.

Remember earlier when I mentioned that phrase "similarities rather than differences" back in Chapter Eight? The similarity between that alcoholic and me was that I smoked marijuana the way that alcoholic drank. I was the kind of marijuana addict who smoked before I got out of bed in the morning, and I smoked every chance I got throughout the day, just like that alcoholic drank. Our substances were different, but our actions and the results were the same. I've learned since then that I can get a lot out of any twelve-step meeting I attend if I remember to replace their substance with mine and listen for those similarities.

**FELLOWSHIP, noun** *fe·lə·ship\*
**Definition of fellowship**, from Webster's New World College Dictionary, Fifth Edition
**1:** companionship; company.

During the meetings, we share experiences, strengths and hope with each other. But before and after the meetings and at events, we also share community and friendship. Connection with another human being is the most essential part of being human, I think. Newborn babies require human contact, or they do not thrive. They die. This requirement doesn't change as we get older. I spent many years hiding behind the invisible wall I'd created and reinforced with marijuana and other substances. I separated myself from others, and my soul—my spirit—was dying. I was certainly not thriving. In order to thrive, I, too, need engagement with other humans, healthy humans, to feel connected to something larger than myself—the universe. Today I want friends, people who know me and understand me and share similar interests beyond being recovering addicts. I must do my part in that relationship building. It starts with me reaching out, letting my guard down—just a little—and getting to know others, and letting others get to know me.

One way that I did that was by joining in. I learned about meetings *before* the meeting. Arriving at the meeting room early, I could meet others who also showed up early before the meeting started. Maybe they had a service commitment at the meeting, were dropped off by a friend or family member, or just liked showing up early too. I'd say "Hi," and they'd say "Hi," and we'd get to talking. It was awkward at first every time I met someone new; sometimes, it's still awkward. But, no matter how uncomfortable I felt, I'd start the same every time, "Hi, I'm Kathy. How are you doing?" Slowly, I got to know people. Some people I met I'd seek out again outside of the meetings, and others I only spoke with during meetings.

Soon I also discovered meetings *after* the meeting. After the last prayer, the official meeting breaks up. People gather in small groups, maybe talking about what they heard in the meeting, catching up, or getting to know each other a little better. I spent many evenings after the meetings talking for hours, literally, in the parking lot of the meeting place or going to a late dinner and talking in the restaurant parking lot. I felt so connected to some of those people that I never wanted those moments to end.

The first event I attended was a housewarming party. I showed up early, and eventually, other people showed up. One man arrived, and I recognized him from the Friday meeting. He was kind, said hi, asked me how I was doing, and we had a conversation. Like adults. Without getting high. And it was great. I remember feeling comfortable, at ease, and accepted.

Another important part of fellowship and friendship is getting phone numbers and using those numbers. Making phone calls to reach out and make connection seems to be the hardest thing any of us does. I'll tell you the secret that helped me pick up that phone and call another member when I was new. I'd call someone while praying they didn't answer, and when they answered, I'd say, "Hi, this is Kathy. I'm practicing this reaching out thing I've heard about, and I have absolutely no idea what to say next."

Whoever I called would take over and share a little about themselves—we all love talking about ourselves—and then they'd ask me a question, and then we'd be talking to each other. It was magical how naturally the conversation flowed. It still is.

All these actions—attending meetings, participating in fellowship, and making new connections—provided opportunities that helped me to become a more complete human being, active in my life and my recovery instead of sitting on the sidelines.

Now that you know about going through that detox phase, it will most likely happen while you are attending meetings. Please know the other members will understand when you are having a rough day or if you cry consistently throughout the meeting, week after week. You can share about it, and they will understand even better. I've shared a little about the mindset needed to move forward, how and where to find your people, group, or tribe, what to expect in meetings, and what fellowship is all about.

I've heard it suggested that new members attend several meetings a week; some members even suggest ninety meetings in ninety days. I suggest you do what works for you and your schedule. If you have a job or a family, you might do one a day or three a week in the evenings. If you are unemployed, you might try a meeting or two every day.

When I started out, I attended one meeting a week. Eventually, I attended two meetings a week. I didn't experience significant growth during my early recovery because I didn't put much effort into my early recovery. It took me a long time to learn how to apply the principles and tools I was learning. You can do it your way or do it the suggested way. However, if you choose to go for it, once you have a consistent meeting schedule, the next step is finding a dedicated guide—called a sponsor—to show you the ropes.

# CHAPTER THIRTEEN

# Finding A Guide

*I* used to think I could work the steps in the workbooks without any help, but now I know I need the experience of someone who has been around a little while and already worked the steps to help me out.

I alluded to this previously, but in case you've forgotten, when I began my sobriety, I was not looking for recovery. I didn't know what recovery meant, much less how it differed from sobriety. But I did know I had been miserable smoking marijuana, my life had become unmanageable in every sense of the word, and I wanted a solution. However, up to that point in my life, the only person I knew I could mostly count on was myself, and while it wasn't a *great* starting point, it *was* a starting point. My second husband wasn't interested in listening, learning, or providing the support I needed. Before attending in-person recovery support meetings, I knew very little about the structure of a twelve-step program.

I initially chose recovery to get the law off my back, avoid prison, and learn to smoke weed in moderation.

After my arrest, I conducted hours of internet research to learn more about marijuana use, addiction, and anything related to my situation. I was looking for the loophole. I discovered many things about marijuana, THC, and the brain. I learned that marijuana was a depressant; it slowed my thoughts and my actions. My experience was that weed gave me more focus and that I accomplished more when I was high. I didn't feel like it was a depressant; it gave me superpowers. The idea that smoking had become a problem baffled me.

While attending online chat room meetings, I found out I could order workbooks for each step and work on the steps all by myself. I'd learned to rely on my smarts to get me through life, and I thought this was pretty smart. I ordered the Step One workbook, and when it arrived, I dug in. For a minute, things got better. I was honest with myself about my substance abuse, answering all the questions to the best of my ability. Putting pen to paper helped me to remember all sorts of situations I'd put myself in and embarrassing times I'd rather not have remembered. By the end of that first workbook, I had a much clearer picture of my relationship with mind- and mood-altering substances. Frankly, it also depressed the hell out of me. It was obvious, however, that I had a problem. More than I ever imagined.

I completed the Step Two and Step Three workbooks in the same fashion. I'd also started attending in-person meetings and listening to others speak. The subject of a sponsor came up in many shares, and I gathered I had to *ask* someone to be my sponsor; they didn't just volunteer. It was also suggested to have a sponsor of the same sex as myself to avoid any infatuations or distractions. That was a good suggestion. Although I made it through the workbooks on my own, I eventually realized I wanted and needed a sponsor to lead me through the twelve steps and teach me about the principles, someone who had already completed their steps, someone whose life appeared to be evolving, moving forward in a positive direction.

I had gone far too long in the rooms of recovery without a sponsor. My obstacle? For the most part, women did not attend the meetings I attended. Funny how, when I was using,

I hung out in a man cave full of guys whose last names I didn't know, and now I was not using in a room full of guys whose last names I didn't know.

My saving grace was that I was desperate; apparently, desperation is a valuable asset when entering recovery. I was miserable. Sobriety without recovery for me meant wildly shifting emotions, a snarky attitude, unpredictable depression, and *zero* coping skills. My answer for handling life's challenges for twenty-plus years was to "get high," and I wasn't doing that now.

Among the suggestions I'd heard in meetings was this gem, "Select a sponsor who has what you want."

Well, I had no idea what I wanted—I only knew what I didn't want anymore. I didn't want to feel like crap every day, behave like a child when life got hard, or continue to do everything for everybody else without regard for my own needs.

Anybody with a little more time than I had seemed to be dealing with life better than I was. Therefore, almost everyone in the recovery rooms had what I wanted—serenity amid life's daily challenges, a solution to the problem of living.

Potential sponsor criteria included someone who appeared to be happy to be clean and sober, was actively living a program of recovery, attended meetings regularly, had a sponsor of their own, and had worked all the steps.

Following these suggestions and paying attention during the meetings, one potential sponsor came to mind, but this person was a man. He attended the meetings weekly and carried a beat-up old Big Book held together with a couple of rubber bands. He quoted from that book when sharing examples of how he applied the principles he'd learned to his life—much like that pastor I once heard. He seemed serene and laid back. He talked about his sponsor, and he sponsored others. I showed up one Friday night ready to ask him to be my sponsor because I needed a sponsor before I did something self-destructive, like smoke again.

Arriving early to the meeting, I waited for my future sponsor to show up. Instead, another sober guy showed up first to open the room and make the coffee. I started with small talk, and then I told him that I'd finally picked someone to be my sponsor. I also shared who. He paused and looked at me quietly for a moment, walked to the front of the room, grabbed a phone list and handed it to me. He suggested that I call a woman he pointed out on the list before I asked the person I'd selected. I felt like all the air had been let out of my balloon. It was hard to work up the courage to ask someone to be my sponsor—I wanted to get it over with before I lost my nerve. But I had learned just enough to take a suggestion, and if I didn't like what I heard from the woman he suggested, I could still come back to the meeting the next week and ask my intended target to be my sponsor.

Long story short, I called the woman and arranged a time to speak with her. We spent over an hour talking, and at the end of that call, I had my first sponsor. It isn't necessary to have anything in common with the person who sponsors you except a desire to stay sober and grow as a human being, but she and I had a lot in common at the time. We began with Step One. Even though I had finished the first three steps in those workbooks, she wanted to guide me from the beginning. I was disappointed but agreed because I really didn't know what I was doing, and she had done this before.

Looking back, asking her to be my sponsor regularly brought her back into the room. When someone asks me to sponsor, I, too, tend to show up more consistently at meetings they attend.

A sponsor's role in the recovery process is very simple. They are not a friend, though they can become a friend or may already be a friend. A sponsor's purpose is to lead others through learning the steps, just like they learned the steps from their sponsor. That's it. Everything else I got from my sponsors was icing on the cake. I learned a lot, too, about how to be a mother, a daughter, a sister, a wife, an employee, a co-worker, and a friend.

Sponsors share their experience, strength and hope with their sponsees, the "student" learning the steps. Sponsors celebrate milestones with us and encourage further growth.

Each of my sponsors knows everything about me—*everything*—and they love me and accept me as I am. My sponsor is usually the first person I call when facing a challenge.

That wasn't always the case.

The first time I faced a real challenge in recovery, I did what I'd always done—figured it out on my own. I used all the tools and teachings I'd gotten up to that point, but I didn't ask for help. I worked it out *then* I called my sponsor. I thought to myself, *She's going to be so proud of me, getting through this challenge all by myself.*

You know what she said after I'd relayed the whole tale, beaming to myself?

She said, "Why didn't you call me first?"

I was surprised and a little embarrassed. I explained that I'd figured it out. She replied that I didn't need to do life alone anymore, and she strongly suggested that I call her first the next time I had a problem and run my thought process by her. She continued, saying that the solution I came up with worked for my situation, but I didn't know it would at the time. I could hear and respect what she was saying. I *had* asked her to be my sponsor, and I was allowed to take advantage of her experience and wisdom, which was more extensive than my own at the time. It was difficult at first to learn to stop, pause, and reach out. It took practice. I still stumble when I ask others for help.

The sponsor leads, and I follow. I take action, ask for homework concerning whatever step we are working on, then do the work. Maybe the assignment is reading literature, answering questions in a workbook, or even doing a writing exercise my sponsor feels will help reveal more to me about me. That's *my* role in my recovery. I do the work by taking the action suggested.

Some people have the same sponsor from day one until one of them dies. Other times, for a variety of reasons, people change sponsors. There came a time when I needed to find a new sponsor.

First, I searched for a new sponsor. Then I prayed to my higher power about my choice, wrote about my whys and my feelings, and checked my motives for changing sponsors and for choosing the person I selected. Finally, I asked the new person and lovingly let go of the current sponsor. I became a stronger person during that process, maturing a little more. I learned to practice courage, compassion, empathy, and tolerance. I was clear about my intentions and moved from the former relationship into the new one without making a mess. *Who was this person acting like an adult, facing the issue instead of running?!* The newer version of me!

As with many things in life, selecting a sponsor is simple, but it's not easy. To review, I attended the same meetings for three or more weeks, watched and listened, and wrote down the names of anyone whose story resonated with me. When approaching prospective sponsors, it's okay to have criteria or questions. Criteria might include asking if the prospect has a sponsor, if they have completed all the steps, if there are other meetings they also attend regularly, and maybe a schedule of when they are usually available. I had one person on my list, but others may have a few, and you need to ask each person until one who meets the criteria says yes.

I once heard a man share about his sponsor dying. His sponsor told him, "You need to find another sponsor without delay. You cannot be left unsupervised." I absolutely believe that to be true for me. I've come up with some amazing, justifiable thinking that dissolved when run by another person, and the best people I've found to run stuff by are those who will *not* tell me what I want to hear. They will tell me—with love, compassion, and empathy—what I *need* to hear.

When my second sponsor died of cancer in 2018, I was without a sponsor for a very short time, yet I was always looking, always listening. I picked a woman to be my temporary sponsor—remember, I know that I can't be left unsupervised—and I kept searching for the sponsor I have today.

Up to now, I've attended regular meetings regularly, I've taken a meeting commitment, which we'll discuss in detail in a later chapter on service, I have a sponsor, and my mindset is clear. Change was slowly taking place within me, and I had to decide if I was willing to keep changing. Change is the only constant in life, and a lot of change comes with the decision to embark on the road to addiction recovery.

# CHAPTER FOURTEEN

# Changing Our Surroundings

*"There are two things addicts hate: change, and things remaining the same."*

The first time I heard this phrase, I laughed because, for me, it was true. I wanted to keep things the way they were. I wanted to be able to use marijuana like before, and I wanted to be able to hang out with my using friends, continuing what I believed were the good times.

But I also wanted my life to get better. I wanted to own a house, finish my college degree, and be the same person around everyone with no more perpetually maintained secrets or lies. I wanted to go on real vacations to places I'd never been, have great adventures, and make new memories.

I wanted life both ways. To change a little but also to stay the same.

I didn't get what I wanted. I got so much more, and I am grateful every day.

In my early sobriety, a result of the felony charge, I explained to my using buddies that I had to stop "for a while" and jump through some hoops so the court would clear my charges. Time passed—the program I agreed to follow lasted for eighteen months—and while I continued to visit those friends, things got different. During my visits, at some point in the evening, they all disappeared to the backyard to smoke weed, leaving me alone in the garage with a pool cue in my hand. One of my friends even gave someone a rash of shit when they lit up a joint in my presence. I was touched at first. But as my head cleared more and more, I started to realize something I'd never considered before. I no longer had something they wanted. I didn't bring beer to the party anymore, I didn't buy weed, and I didn't smoke anyone out. I wasn't one of the gang anymore. We had nothing else in common when the weed and the booze were removed from the equation. We had years of history, but it all centered around alcohol, drugs, and parties. I was an outsider. Now I began to feel as uncomfortable visiting that house as they must have felt when I came to visit. Because we weren't really friends. We were using buddies—as in, we used each other to get high and keep up the illusion that all was right in our world.

Once, while I was still smoking weed, the thought popped into my head that I didn't know the last name of most in that group of smoking buddies. One guy's first name was the city he was from. I knew the last name of the homeowner but none of the others. I'd been hanging out with these people for over eight years, and they were strangers.

Soon I was attending regular meetings and wasn't having fun visiting those old friends. I decided to do an experiment. I wasn't going to call those using buddies for a while. I wondered how much time would pass before I received a call from any of them. I came to realize that I was always the one reaching out, inviting myself over, or setting up beach parties or camping trips. So, I took a break. You probably guessed the outcome of this experiment. I never got a call. Not from that day to this one.

A popular phrase heard in the meetings was that we only needed to change one thing, and that was everything. We needed to change our playgrounds—where we hung out to smoke. Change our playmates—those pot-smoking friends. Change our playthings—the bongs, pipes, and other accumulated paraphernalia.

I learned to fill the void with new, healthier people, places and things that supported my new life choices. I found new places to hang out with new, sober people.

I know many people who, early in their recovery, chose to remain friends with their using buddies. This is not the case with all addicts or alcoholics. Many started using with their friends in grade school or high school, and they kept in touch with their friends long after they got clean and sober. That's not my story, though.

There is a saying that goes something like this; if you hang out in a barber shop long enough, you are going to get a haircut. Some members have returned to the rooms, sharing that they hung out with their using friends one joint too long. Others continued to practice their recovery programs, and some of their friends liked what they saw and got clean and sober, too. Everyone is different. I know I have no desire to be around people who use marijuana. That's not a safe place for me to be.

And the way I learned to change my habits and behaviors was by learning what those twelve steps are all about.

# CHAPTER FIFTEEN

## The Steps to Restoration

*I* practice the twelve steps of recovery founded by Alcoholics Anonymous and adopted by Marijuana Anonymous. That's where I got sober, and it works for me. I've heard about several other programs over the years, and people seem to be getting sober by other means as well. I can only share my experience, and twelve-step recovery is my experience.

When I have my heart set on something and the outcome is not what I expected, I feel disappointed. Emotional immaturity is when, in my disappointment, I pout—literally pout—because I didn't get my way. Once, not long ago, I was not a graceful loser. I'd use all the old tools at my disposal to express my disappointment, much like a child, by manipulating with tears and engaging in the silent treatment or giving someone the cold shoulder. If confronted, I'd slam things down on counters, slam doors to express my displeasure, and deny that I was upset.

I was also egocentric or self-centered. I've learned that this means I thought of myself first and foremost, and others maybe. I could be inconsiderate, selfish, intolerant, and needy at times. I lacked compassion. I also had a poor filter when speaking with others.

My tools—those coping mechanisms I learned while growing up to navigate safely through life—were rusty and outdated. I needed some new tools, and I didn't have a clue how to develop new behaviors and habits or how to act like an adult in the world.

It's been suggested that when a person begins to use marijuana, their emotional growth is put on pause—stunted—at whatever age they begin using. The body grows, but the mind, the thoughts, and the social skills remain at that age when the marijuana use began. Many people share that they started smoking or using marijuana at an early age, usually twelve. Fewer people, like myself, didn't start using marijuana until the age of eighteen or older.

Imagine a grown human, at thirty-eight, still responding to life's challenges like a twelve-year-old or an eighteen-year-old. I was an adult woman nearing the age of forty who behaved like a child when I didn't get my way. When I got clean and sober, I resumed the process of growing up, and for every year that I stayed sober and worked those steps of recovery, I matured a little more. I needed to catch up to the age I actually was, but at an emotional level. I didn't know how to do this. How would I change my thinking and behavior to catch up with myself?

First, I had to rebuild my thinking and my behavior.

Imagine a beat-up old car, rusted, maybe with flat tires and a broken windshield. Bad shape, but not beyond saving. Some steps need to be taken to bring that rusty old heap back to life before it can be useful again.

Same goes for us, for me. I was much like the beat-up old truck rusting out in a field. I required some tender loving care. This is where those twelve steps and their lessons came in. Those twelve steps are the program of recovery. My sponsor helped me to walk through each step, learn the principle or value the step represented as well as where, when, and how to apply it, so I could clear the wreckage I'd created and develop a new set of tools for living life on life's terms.

Step One, surrendering, helped me see that try as I might, I could not control my marijuana use through sheer willpower, and when I attempted to do so, my life spun out of control and became unmanageable.

I regularly hear that Step One is the only step we have to do perfectly.

Step One has two parts: admitting that we are powerless over marijuana and admitting that life has become unmanageable.

I had to admit to myself that I'd been trying to control the uncontrollable, and in doing so, my life became unmanageable. Over time, trying to control everything outside of myself and neglecting my innermost self, I ended up rusting in a field, just like that truck.

Every person I've met who could admit both parts—powerlessness and unmanageability—honestly, in their hearts, begins the journey of restoration.

Step Two, hope, was practiced when I came to believe I might find someone or something with more knowledge about restoring old trucks or repairing spirits than I had. Maybe a master mechanic, a power greater than ourselves.

Step Three, faith, was learned when I decided to relinquish my will and my life—my thoughts and my actions—to a power greater than me. I reached out, admitting my lack of knowledge in living life on life's terms, and I asked to be restored, trusting that the master mechanic had my best interests at heart.

Step Four, courage, required making a list of all the stuff that needed to be fixed so that truck could be rebuilt, run smoothly, and look amazing. All of it, from the rat's nest in the engine block to the bird's nest in the rusted-out exhaust pipe.

*All this is a parable for my journey through the recovery steps, so bear with me.*

I also included a list of the items in good condition, so I had a complete inventory, a starting point. Now I've made a list of things that need repair and things that are in good shape.

I met with the master mechanic and another friend, in this case, my sponsor, and read my list of items to the friend, who helped me refine the list and clarify as needed. I began seeing how the old rusty truck became an object of neglect by looking at my contribution, my part in the relationship. Maybe I skipped the various check-ups or ignored that loud sound when I started it up, and while the seats aren't as bad as I think, I can admit that the cracked windshield needs replacing.

That's the lesson of Step Five, integrity, sharing the list with a neutral and knowledgeable third party to ensure the list is thorough and accurate before proceeding to the next phase of restoration.

The steps are in this order for a reason. We wouldn't put new rims and tires on a car if the axle is shot.

Step Six, willingness, represents the pause between acknowledging work to be done and preparing to ask for the help required to improve the truck's condition. I am about to change how the truck looks, feels, and runs. I asked myself, *Am I ready for this? Am I ready to get rid of the rust and the torn interior and clean this truck up?* When I became even a little bit ready, I practiced willingness.

Step Seven, humility, is the act of asking the master mechanic for help to begin restoring the truck. This is a challenging step because maybe up to now, self-reliance was my go-to, figuring out life myself or giving up when life got too hard. Now I invite others into my life who have already restored a truck. I follow their examples, look at the truck daily, and make little changes to restore my values, replacing worn-out ones with ones that work and slowly rebuild the truck to a working condition.

Step Eight, forgiveness, is when I gave myself a break and practiced self-forgiveness. It took years of neglect and elementary coping skills before that truck ended up in its current state of disrepair. But to create change, I realized the restoration is on me. Blame delays healing and growing. So, I learned to forgive myself for not seeing how bad life had gotten, and I forgave myself for not getting better sooner. We get it when we get it, each of us. Then I made a new list of all the damaged parts and to whom I've caused harm. I included how I might approach the same circumstance differently in the future should it arise again, and I became willing to make those amends—apologies coupled with changes in my behavior.

Step Nine, discipline; I slowly made amends to others one by one, letting each know that *I knew* how I messed up, that I felt remorse, and vowed to do my best every day not to practice those harmful actions again. I also learned to respond to the same situations differently in the future.

Step Ten, perseverance, is consistent maintenance of that restored vehicle. I check the oil, wash the exterior and vacuum the interior. I perform all the actions that keep the truck in good shape. To continue with the restoration theme, if the truck gets a flat tire, I repair it immediately now instead of driving around on the spare for months. In a real-life situation, when my tone is sharp and unkind, I can stop and correct my behavior on the spot. Acknowledging my harms in each relationship brings it into the light. No longer carrying the burden, I am able to move forward in life, restoring my spirit to serve its true purpose.

Step Eleven, spirituality; I maintain my relationship with the master mechanic. I may need to ask for help in the future, and this relationship is essential to keeping my head and being helpful to others.

How does one maintain or grow a relationship with another? By reaching out, checking in, and remembering that back in Step Three I asked to be restored. In this step, I want to maintain that connection with the one who restored me.

Life continues to happen. I need to know that my relationship with the master mechanic is solid when life throws me a curve ball. I might get rear-ended, or I might be the cause. I am more likely to remain calm and levelheaded, knowing what to do next when my relationship with the master mechanic is solid. I stay in constant contact through prayer and meditation.

Prayer is as simple as talking with my higher power like I'd talk to a trusted friend, and meditation is the act of becoming still and quiet, listening for the guidance I asked for in prayer. The answers rarely come right away, but they do come.

Step Twelve, the principle of service, is when I let other people who may have a rusty old truck hear about how I restored mine. I don't tell them that they should do what I did. I teach by example, and I practice the principles of these steps every day so that my example is seen rather than heard. If someone likes the look and the sound of my restored "truck," maybe they want a little assistance restoring their truck, too. All these steps, the values I've restored or instilled for the first time, helped to accelerate my emotional maturity. I give away what I've learned to anyone who asks, and in doing so, I keep what I've learned for one more day by reinforcement through repetition. I avoid telling anyone what to do or giving unsolicited advice.

The concept of service evolves for everyone. The most restorative part of recovery is in being of service to others. Let's explore what service looks like in the rooms of recovery and out in the world.

# CHAPTER SIXTEEN

## From Selfish and Self-Seeking to Selfless Service

> *Everything good that has happened*
> *to me has happened as a direct*
> *result of helping someone else.*
> —*Danny T.*

In a recovery program, being of service means carrying the message that anyone can have a spiritual awakening—can get clean and sober and stay clean and sober—by taking the steps with an experienced guide. We also practice the principles outlined in the previous chapter daily in *all* of our affairs.

I was the product of absent parents. They were there physically. They just weren't *there,* weren't present. In doing all that I could as a child to earn their love, I became a perfectionist. I was seeking a payoff—acceptance, attention, acknowledgment, love—anything that resembled the family units I saw portrayed in 1960s television shows.

As I got older, my manipulative, people-pleasing nature improved, and when I started smoking weed, it was very important to me that my new hobby was consistently supported. I gave of myself however and whenever I could. I brought the best gifts and thought of everyone, keeping track of birthdays and anniversaries, not only for my immediate family but for as far as my circle of influence reached. I also heavily compromised or destroyed those Sunday school values I once had to support my habit. I was under the false impression that my kindness was well-received. Each person seemed pleasantly impressed with my thoughtfulness. This backfired, though, because I was a selfish, self-centered person who hung out with selfish, self-centered people. My thoughtful generosity was not returned—an expectation on my part, to be sure, but still—and now those acquaintances expected my generosity and kindness. I believed that I had to continue my actions, or they'd desert me. And I did not want to be abandoned, even by those fair-weather friends. I eventually learned to stop behaving in that manipulative, people-pleasing manner, and those people disappeared. The world didn't end, though. The universe was making room for a better quality of friends.

I lived a life I'd created for myself where I had to give so I could get, except that I wasn't giving love, acceptance, or compassion. I taught people how to treat me, and they didn't treat me with love and respect. I did a lot of giving of gifts and time but didn't receive much in return, except marijuana. But that was the result I was ultimately seeking; that was my motive.

My friendships weren't really friendships. They were business deals, private negotiations, and I had numerous associates.

I lived that way for years, building connections so I would always have what I needed. It didn't always pan out that way, though.

## From Selfish and Self-Seeking to Selfless Service

When I first heard people share about service, I thought I had been of service too, but I began to see I was just manipulating others to get what I wanted.

When I chose to be sober and attend meetings—it was a choice as alternatively, I could have gone to prison—I was still utilizing all of my old coping mechanisms. I just didn't know it yet. The skills I used with using buddies didn't work the same with self-aware people, those with confidence and positive self-esteem. These recovering addicts and alcoholics didn't need anything from me, and they didn't want anything from me. Frankly, when I got to the rooms of recovery, I didn't have anything the healthy, sober people wanted.

Still, early in my recovery, when I heard about being of service through taking meeting commitments, I thought, *Here's where I'll shine, and they will see how valuable I can be.* I was still looking to get something in return for giving—acceptance, a feeling of belonging, a pat on the back. I knew how I'd gotten attention before. I'd do the same thing here–I'd become invaluable, and then I'd be appreciated and accepted.

I did a great job as the literature person, but so did other people. I didn't yet understand that the purpose of service in the twelve-step community was to carry the message and to keep the doors open for the next new person who arrived. Those who came before kept the candles burning in the darkness for those who come later, so to speak.

It took me a long time to realize I needed to examine my motives when I wanted to do something for someone else. One of the things I found attractive about the twelve-step community was that no one wanted anything from me. Not my body, my money, my stuff, or my weed. They wanted to be able to share their stories with kindred spirits so they could stay sober another twenty-four hours. That was it. The people who rotated through the service positions were the lighthouse keepers, keeping the ships from hitting the rocks so the passengers could safely make it to shore.

A big part of service in recovery is to focus on self *less*. When I'm helping someone set up the chairs in a meeting, I am not thinking about myself. When I put out the literature for the other members to take, I am not thinking about myself. When I make the coffee for a meeting, I am not thinking about myself—actually, I'm wondering how people can drink coffee at 7:45 in the evening and function the following morning.

As time passed, I learned about new levels of service. Service appears to start when we show up at the meeting. The long-timers and short-timers need the newcomers to fill the seats so they have someone to tell their stories to in the meeting, and the newcomers serve to remind those with some time what it's like out there because people tend to forget. When anyone shares their story, they are of service to everyone else in the meeting.

Meeting commitments are the next level of service. Members volunteer to help keep the meeting going. All positions rotate, at every level, so that everybody receives a turn and is given an opportunity to participate in supporting their meetings. It's been my experience that most meeting commitments are six months long. Then elections take place, and new people take a turn.

Sponsors provide service by leading newcomers through the steps. This process is a two-way opportunity. The newcomer learns about the steps, the principles, and themselves while sharing their story with a sponsor, and the sponsor gets to work all the steps again, sharing their own story and learning a little bit more about themselves, too. I've personally worked all the steps with over a dozen sponsees at least once, and I learn something new about myself every time. Sometimes I am reminded of some event or behavior I've forgotten that I haven't addressed yet.

## From Selfish and Self-Seeking to Selfless Service

When I arrived in the rooms of recovery, I did not have the capacity to face all the pain I had caused or received. Looking back on it, I believe that my higher power revealed only as much as I was capable of handling. As my capacity to deal with the wreckage of my past grew, more memories were revealed to me through the stories that others shared. Slowly I was reminded of issues, circumstances, feelings and emotions that I still needed to process. My sponsor and I worked through those things together when I was ready for more. As time passes, more is revealed, still.

The service structure of all the anonymous groups I've participated in looks like an inverted pyramid or triangle. Members reside at the top or widest part of this upside-down triangle, supported by the group or meetings, which in turn are supported by the districts that are supported by World Services. Service opportunities exist at all levels, and most of those positions rotate every six months to a year. The district meetings are where members discuss the business of the various weekly meetings in their district and where each meeting's group representatives obtain literature, chips, and information about events and World Service issues they then take back to their meetings.

Having served in several district-level service positions, I've learned a great deal about how I interact within a group. I've learned how to disagree without arguing, how to honor a commitment, and how to step down when my time was up. I've also learned not to take other people's personalities personally, even when they want to make things personal. I've even learned how to give back to a larger group and learn some humility while doing it.

World Services serves to carry the message of recovery out into the world and support districts by maintaining a website with meeting listings, literature that provides a general overview of what recovery in the twelve-step community is all about, as well as manning phone lines for those who are brave enough or desperate enough to reach out. All these things help practicing addicts find recovery rooms.

Service work opportunities are all around us as we move through the day. We might recognize them, or we might not. I think of service work as any selfless act. I don't do it to get recognition or awards. I do it because it needs to be done.

A woman in one of the meetings I've attended often shares about returning the shopping cart. It's a simple act, but it makes an impact that can change the world. Taking a cart back to its corral takes a little more time—probably a whole fifteen seconds or so—and is a simple act of service. And it's kinder to do than to leave the cart in the middle of a parking space or parked in a planter.

Every day we're presented with hundreds of ways we can make the world a slightly better place than when it was when we got up this morning. Hold a door open for someone. Smile. Allow someone with fewer groceries to go ahead of us in the line. Pick up some trash while walking through a park or down a street. It goes on and on. I keep my eyes open for anything I can do to make my world a better place. Not for you, or even for me, but because I know that it's the right thing to do, for all of us, and because I spent so many years doing the opposite.

If you decide to give this recovery thing a try, and you attend the same meeting for more than six months, you might consider taking a service position. Not for the pat on the back or to show people how wonderful and giving you are, but instead to give back or pay forward what was so freely given so the light is still on when the next person arrives.

## PART THREE

# Recovery Is Simple, but It's Not Easy

Getting sober is easy. Staying sober is hard, especially in the beginning. I was great at quitting. I was also great at starting up again the minute I experienced any level of emotional turmoil.

Recovery is simple, but it isn't easy. A recovery program offered me a step-by-step set of directions, along with a guide, to develop a set of tools for living that help me to stay sober when life becomes challenging. Simple.

All I had to do was ask. Not easy.

A few things still trip me up, though, if I am not vigilant in my personal spiritual and emotional development in sobriety. I might forget how miserable I felt, focusing instead on bitter resentment, wishing for the "good old days." I might forget the illusions and lies I tried to maintain for others while using marijuana. I might fall back on old behaviors, living life on my terms instead of following the principles outlined in the twelve-step program. And, in resting on my laurels—working the recovery program just enough to get comfortable in life—I stop going to meetings, stop reaching out to others, and instead attempt to resume life on my terms, forgetting how I got this blessed life in the first place.

The gifts I received in recovery were not the gifts I expected when I got here. I also experienced a great deal of self-pity, feeling that I had wasted twenty-plus years of my life floating in a boat, ignoring the oars. The people in the rooms of recovery smiled a lot, laughed at themselves, and seemed to be successful. Many had healthy, mature relationships, reliable vehicles, homes, and college degrees. They seemed comfortable in their skin, not awkward or lacking confidence. When I got here, I wanted to get my hands on the stuff and the things. What I have today is so much better than anything tangible. But it took me a while to figure out what they really had and what I really wanted out of life. I had a few things to learn along the way.

## CHAPTER SEVENTEEN

# Avoid Romancing the Stone

I used to think I was immune to the temptation of using marijuana again, but now I know that I only have the next twenty-four hours.

When I hear people share about what life was like, talking about or thinking about all the "fun" times, sharing how good it still smells when the scent of weed drifts by on the breeze, or wondering just how long one can go without using marijuana before being able to use it again, but moderately this time—that's romancing it, making it sound like using marijuana could be good again someday.

My vision for the future may sound familiar to you. I was looking forward to retirement, to the time when I could sit on my porch in my rocking chair smoking weed all day, without a care in the world, watching the world go by. I also thought I was the only person who ever had this thought, and yet, I have heard this exact same vision shared by many people who've gathered in the rooms of recovery. Maybe you have a similar vision.

Before I got arrested, even while I wanted freedom from weed, I never entertained the idea that I would stop smoking weed forever. I'd planned my entire life around using it. Everything in my life was dictated by cannabis—who I hung out with, where I went on vacation, events I attended, and jobs I held.

Earlier I used a barber shop analogy. If I hang out with people using marijuana long enough, eventually, I will probably use marijuana, too. But the opposite is also true. If I hang out with people practicing a program of addiction recovery and living their best lives, I'm more likely also to live my best life in recovery.

I am going to share this sobering thought—no pun intended:

**Sobriety is not a guarantee, even if we do all the suggestions.**

Relapse is a fancy word for going back to using marijuana. Some people say, "so and so has gone out." Other people call it "doing more research." As I'll share in the next chapter, life has offered me many opportunities to start using marijuana again to change my reality. I haven't given in to those opportunities—yet.

I've personally heard hundreds of stories from people who relapse and return to the rooms and share about it. The main theme of all those shares is that the relapse started way before they used the drug.

There's a saying I've heard that goes like this: people who stop going to meetings don't hear what happens to people who stop going to meetings.

People get sober, then work a program of recovery. Maybe they got through half of their steps, maybe all the steps. A new and exciting life began to emerge. Relationships start, improve, or end. Maybe a member gets promoted or signs up for college classes. Gradually, they attend fewer and fewer meetings. Life starts picking up, moving faster. Sober a while, they stop connecting with others in recovery. I've personally heard people on this path tell me that "as soon as they finish the course," or "settle into the new job," or "the new relationship is established," they'll start attending meetings more, call more, or participate more. And then those people cancel more commitments than they honor. They practice more self-pity over what they don't have than gratitude for what they have. One day, after a long period of "have you seen so-and-so lately," so-and-so shows up at a meeting, takes a newcomer chip and shares what happened.

Some of the reasons shared after a relapse included a bruised ego—someone hurt their feelings—or they suffered a large disappointment, or life became difficult, justifying their actions with, "You'd use too if you went through what I went through." Some blame others, "If so-and-so had just taken the time to listen to me," or sheer arrogance, "I've been sober this long—nothing can touch me."

During my first nine months, I relapsed three times. The first time, I experienced that inflated feeling of being certain that I could handle it now—that I could smoke in moderation. I'd been clean for almost two months; surely one joint would be okay. I was incorrect about that. The second time, I was in emotional turmoil. Life got tough, and I didn't like how I felt—marijuana changed that. The final time, I was looking for someone to blame when I started up at the beginning of a road trip.

Once I'd gathered some time, I became a little self-righteous and distanced myself from those people who would relapse again and again. I'm an addict, and when I was finally done for good, I didn't use again, no matter what. That arrogant, self-righteous voice in my head would hear someone share about going out and returning for the fourth or fifth time and think, *if I can do it, with all my stubbornness, why can't those people? If they were done, why did they pick up again? What could be so awful that they felt the need to escape from it, to lose those days they had?* And finally, *if they weren't done, why did they show up at the meetings in the first place?*

I'd forgotten that nothing had to be awful when I was using every hour of every day. Marijuana was just as good for the good times as it was for the bad times. Getting sober leaves a person raw with no tools to handle life on life's terms. The fact that so many addicts and alcoholics choose to get sober in the first place is a miracle. That so many recovering addicts and alcoholics—whose default is to seek relief by changing the way they feel—continue to rack up sober days, months, and years is also a miracle.

Recovery takes work. Daily work. It's not strength that keeps one person sober or lack of strength that sends another person back out. It's the quality of the program they practice. Relapse is as insidious as marijuana addiction, and it happens long before the user picks up the substance. The truth is, seeking relief from my feelings is my natural response to life, my default. It wasn't always drugs—it started with fiction books and television. I always sought a means to avoid uncomfortable feelings. Escaping is how I respond when I don't know how to respond.

If I don't practice my program, self-awareness, and gratitude daily, I'm at risk of relapse. When I don't use the principles, contrary action, connection with others, and resist putting a plan in place, I'm at risk of relapse. If I am not consistently seeking connection to my higher power, I will eventually find a good enough reason or a strong enough "*fuck it*" to justify using weed.

And just for the record, I don't have to use marijuana to distract myself from myself. Right now, while you're reading this, I might be avoiding my feelings by using video streaming, game apps, chores, activity, other people's problems, sex, self-pleasure, reading—anything that will distract me from feeling or dealing with my emotional distress.

When I am in a meeting, I focus on sharing the solution and how I stay sober today. I carry the message that working the steps and being of service will keep me sober. I only share "the mess" —which might be what a shit day I had and how much I hate everybody and everything—if I can end my share with the solution, how I practiced the steps to change my attitude to one of gratitude. I share how I practice recovery when life gets hard instead of how I let life win.

The point of this chapter is to let you know that I am as close to relapse as anyone else. I only have the next twenty-four hours. When I have a solid connection with my higher power, when I practice acceptance of what is in this moment, and when I am of service to others, my chance of staying sober until my head hits the pillow tonight is pretty good.

If I "romance" old tales of my using days, I may set myself up for a relapse. And relapse is a return to old habits—I may not pick up a substance, but I can always behave as if I had. I must always remember that I chose sobriety because I was miserable in my life, that smoking pot stopped being fun. I discovered I cannot be a joyful, contributing member of my community if I am stoned.

# CHAPTER EIGHTEEN

## Progress Not Perfection

*H*ave you ever taken the Holmes-Rahe Stress Inventory? It's an inventory listing a variety of life's stressful moments, events like buying a house, ending a relationship, graduating from college, filing bankruptcy, or having a baby. Moments like that. Each event is given a rating reflecting the amount of stress it produces. The score, reached by adding up all the stress events one has experienced over the course of a year, determines how likely one is to have a health breakdown.

Therapists and counselors use this test to develop a list of techniques to help patients reduce the severity of their stress responses—basically, tools to help a person live life on life's terms. This is much like recovering addicts using the program's tools to adjust their response to life.

I used to believe the illusion that I was in control, not of everything, but of many things. Now I know that I only have control over my response to circumstances or situations.

Living life on life's terms means that when a circumstance arises, I respond accordingly, taking appropriate action or accepting the circumstance as it is. I've learned to practice the act of gratitude while facing life head-on. I practice being grateful for all the things I have, all the circumstances that challenge me and result in personal growth, and all the things I don't have.

When I was using marijuana, it was as if I had blinders on. I was not living life on life's terms. I was living life on my terms. My terms were, "I'll do what I want when I want." I lived by my own set of rules. I manipulated, intimidated, or pouted when I didn't get the desired result. I held my breath until I got my way, sometimes figuratively and also sometimes literally, like a child. I stole if I deemed it necessary, justified it, and then lied about it.

I believed I had control over the outcome of everything. When a circumstance didn't turn out as I thought it should, I became angry and sullen. I got high, ignoring my emotions because I didn't know how to handle those emotions. I didn't deal with my feelings or my emotions as they occurred. After a while, I'd rage over some small thing, much like a boiler exploding.

This is an example of my behavior while actively using marijuana, living life on *my* terms.

I'm standing in the checkout line at the grocery store, waiting my turn to purchase a gallon of milk, a box of cereal, a loaf of enriched white bread, and a jar of peanut butter. I am at the grocery store at 6:45 in the morning on a Tuesday because the previous night, I made a forty-five-minute round-trip run to my dealer's house to score some weed instead of doing refrigerator inventory. When morning came and the kids were getting ready for school, I realized we had nothing for breakfast or lunch.

So, I'm at the store, and I've reached the register. Smiling, the cashier rings up my order. I swipe my debit card through the payment pad and punch in my pin number. The card is declined. I try again. Again, the card is declined.

My face gets hot, my stomach gets tight, and tears well up in my eyes. I feel embarrassed and worthless. Fear swells up inside me, but instead of being afraid, I get angry. When asked if I have another form of payment, I say something rude to the cashier, and I stomp out of the store like a child throwing a tantrum, swearing at shoppers who get in my way. In my head, I rage as I blame the bank, the husband, the kids. Zero to bitch in seconds, pointing fingers at everyone but myself. I rush home, impatient the entire way. I leave the car running, race into the apartment and grab my checkbook. Luckily, no children see me. I hurry back to the market, fuming, dangerous. I return to the check stand where I left my groceries, only to learn that an efficient stockboy has returned all my items to the shelves. My temper rises further; I'm a volcano about to blow. I run through the store, retrieving all the items again. My attitude, already awful, gets worse, and everyone suffers. I behave like an ass. Back in the checkout line, I write the check, probably throw it toward the cashier, and roughly show her my ID.

Do you get the picture? When I feel afraid, I want to protect myself. My strongest armor back then was anger. Anger provided an instant shield. What was the fear? That I had no money, I couldn't feed my children, and the people behind me in line were casting silent judgment. This is how I interacted with my husband, children, customer service agents, and cashiers when I was angry and when things didn't go my way. Anger protected me by building a wall between you and me, putting distance between us. My illogical brain reasoned that you couldn't get close enough to hurt me emotionally if I threw anger at you. How does that old phrase go? If mama ain't happy, ain't nobody happy. I embodied that phrase like I wrote it.

Vulnerability, something I had no experience with, allows me to connect with you, show you my pain and receive love, compassion, and assistance. Vulnerability is the more difficult of the two responses because it opens us up to being hurt; it exposes us. Anger is quicker and easier but ultimately more devastating to ourselves and others. I've learned that vulnerability requires a strength to practice that anger does not. Anger becomes a bully, and vulnerability requires trust and love and courage. I can bounce back from your rejection and ridicule when I realize you are responding with fear, just like I do. It is more difficult to recover from the aftermath of anger because it's a long walk back from there to vulnerability. After I behave badly, the last thing I want to do is look at my behavior, face those I've harmed, and apologize.

By the time I'd gotten sober, I had a huge list of unresolved resentments, feelings, and emotions I had never dealt with healthily. My new default emotion was underlying anger. I was angry about things I couldn't even remember, buried deep beneath resentment after resentment. I'd lived with this anger for so long that I didn't recognize it as an issue. Other people did, though.

If I wanted to live in a state of serenity and peace in recovery, behaving like a healthy, stable grown-up—and I did—I learned that I needed to revisit all those unresolved emotions and feelings, face them, process them, and clear them out. I learned to uncover, discover, and discard those very old feelings, one at a time.

Around this time, I'd been sober for a while and worked the steps. I'd also been attending some meetings weekly, and I was slowly recovering. Slowly. Starting to have an inkling of what it's like to live life on life's terms, I share this.

One day while reviewing my spending plan and bills, I found an extra charge on my credit card statement, made at an establishment somewhere on the East Coast. The charge was around $300 for a riding saddle I didn't order; I didn't own a horse. I felt fearful that I would have to come up with the money to pay the credit card bill even though it wasn't my charge. Once again, I was afraid.

When I called the credit card company, I felt defensive, as if *I* had done something wrong and gotten caught. I'd done a lot of shady things in my past—petty theft and shoplifting—and that guilt was like a shadow. The customer service representative sounded cold and I wasn't feeling kind. I wanted the charge removed and removed now. I overexplained myself. My tone became self-righteous and arrogant. I knew I should have checked my attitude, but I didn't know how to do that. My attitude negatively affected the representative's attitude. The rep opened a fraud claim and applied a credit to my account; the company would investigate the charge. The rep asked if there was anything else, and when I replied that there was not, the call was abruptly ended.

I felt remorse. I could have handled that call differently. The representative's job was to resolve issues, and the rep did. I called the 800 number back, and surprisingly, the same person answered the call. I humbled myself enough to apologize for my behavior, for speaking to the rep so roughly. I also justified my behavior, but the apology was better than I'd done in the past. My apology was accepted, and the rep said, "Have a nice day." I felt a little better when the call disconnected. Progress.

Life continues to happen, and when I was fifteen months sober, I received a phone call from my mother telling me my maternal grandfather had died. My only experience with death before this was when I was ten and my paternal grandfather died. I was very sad, but when I was ten, there was no talk or discussion of feelings. My parents did not have the tools to handle their own emotions and so could not help me or my brother cope with ours.

When I got this news as an adult, I felt like I'd been punched in the gut. It became difficult to breathe, like my chest carried a heavy weight on my heart. I felt such sorrow, beyond tears, though there were many. To smoke or drink away this heaviest and most painful of feelings, though? No, I knew in my heart to do that would dishonor my grandfather's memory. It would lessen what I felt for him. Instead, I lay on my bed for three days, numb, because I didn't know how to move through grief. Each day the pain lessened a little bit. I stayed sober.

I've lost some other people in my life since then, people very close to my heart—my mother-in-law died of cancer in 2011, and my grandmother followed her two weeks later from Alzheimer's disease when I was eight years sober. I am grateful that by then, I'd worked all the steps and had a solid enough foundation for life's many twists and turns. I didn't think about smoking; instead, I reached out to people who could love me while I grieved.

When I was almost eleven years sober, my mother died of ovarian cancer. My brother and I were entirely present, by her side, for the last thirty-three days of her life. I would like to say that I never thought of smoking or drinking, but I'd be lying. Still, I reached out to people who could listen and love me while I walked through that long month. When I was fourteen years sober, my sponsor died, also of cancer. I didn't need to smoke away feelings then, either. Instead, I could draw from all my experiences when others went through the same situations. I got to be the one who reached out and brought casseroles, sent cards and left supportive, loving voicemail messages because those who came before me taught me through their examples.

Grief, the heaviest emotion, in my opinion, comes in many forms. Divorce, for instance, brings on feelings of grief. Not only do we grieve loss, we also grieve what could have been. When I ended a twenty-year marriage, I lived with self-doubt and shared my feelings with a small circle of support. I did not run from those uncomfortable feelings. Others showed me how to walk with dignity and grace. When others journeyed down similar paths, later on, I was able to share my experience when called upon to do so, providing an ear to listen and comfort during a difficult time.

In January 2018, recreational marijuana use became legal in my state. The sharing in meetings during that year was primarily around the topic of "What to do now that marijuana is legal?" I felt that whether it was legal or not, I am a marijuana addict and cannot use marijuana and retain my freedom. Period.

Several people, however, used legalization as a reason to start smoking again. I am grateful to those people for doing the "research" and returning to the meetings to report that marijuana still didn't work for them. I don't know why anyone thought legalization would make marijuana use less of a problem for them.

Life on life's terms also means I don't compromise my new values, no matter what.

When I was sixteen years sober, the world shut down in a way that few had ever seen. Initially, I thought the world was overreacting, but I kept my sarcasm to myself.

I was getting ready for a big celebration weekend, my fifty-fifth birthday. On March 14, 2020, Disneyland Resort closed, and I expected it would last a couple of weeks. I held an annual pass and loved visiting Disneyland. I remained optimistic it would reopen before my birthday.

That was not the case. All recovery support meeting locations shut down practically overnight—when the recovery community needed them most. Grocery store shelves were emptied of rice, pasta, canned goods, and paper products. A stay-at-home order was issued worldwide. *Worldwide.* Fear filled the hearts of most humans, and there was global uncertainty about what would happen next. People were scared, and people were dying, and me? I was upset that my birthday plans were canceled. The beginning of a "life on my terms" response was brewing.

For a while, I actively practiced the behaviors I'd worked hard to set aside—pettiness, self-centeredness, and passive-aggressive behaviors, to name a few. Depression set in and lasted for a few days. Then someone reached out, calling to remind me about the power of gratitude. I had toilet paper and frozen food. Another person called to share with me what they were grateful to have in their lives—electricity, plenty of water, functioning internet, and someone to be with during lockdown. I was reminded that I *still* had a choice in how I responded. I chose to change my attitude to one of gratitude as well, to look for all the good things. Life on life's terms reestablished itself in my life.

The pandemic shattered my illusion of control in a big way. I realized I was not in control of anything, never had been, and that control of anything and anyone outside myself was an illusion. Once again, I was reminded I only controlled my response to situations and people.

The pandemic provided an opportunity for many marijuana addicts to justify using marijuana again or doubling down on their recovery programs. We are all built differently, and again I was grateful, this time because I wasn't willing to compromise my sobriety. I knew for me that smoking marijuana wouldn't make the pandemic any better.

Instead, I, along with hundreds of others in the recovery community, found a way to get some of our meetings going again using videoconferencing. Most meetings I attended were up and running within a week. We learned together as we went along, we had renewed purpose, and we were being of service for ourselves as much as for anyone else. I offered my knowledge to help others learn how to use videoconferencing.

During the hardest months of the pandemic, a new illness, CHS, emerged in the marijuana community, long-timers became newcomers, and more and more members joined as they realized they were marijuana addicts.

My current husband and I grew closer as a couple. I wrote an addiction recovery journal while I navigated a new landscape of sheltering in place. I still had my ugly moments, but I took responsibility for those moments, and I applied the tools of my program quickly. I made the best of a difficult situation. I leveled up all the tools I'd gathered since starting the twelve-step recovery program. In reality, 2020 was one of the best years of my life in terms of my recovery and my personal development. I certainly had plenty of time on my hands. I learned about myself, grew, and gave back to others.

Living life on life's terms is simple and still not easy. It's about acceptance of what is in this moment. Every moment. Accepting what is does not mean I always approve of what's happening. It only means that I accept what's going on and change what I can, which is usually my attitude. I rise to meet life's challenges with the tools I've gathered practicing my program of recovery.

For the record:

Is life always amazing in recovery? ................ Not always, no.
Do I enjoy all the outcomes? ........................ Nope, I still want what I want.
Am I super excited about every life lesson? ... Hell, no.
Do I continue to hug the cactus? .................. Every day

Hugging the cactus? It means embracing that part of my soul that is ugly, as in "If I hugged the cactus long enough, I would become a [person] of some humility, and that my life would take on a new meaning." Mel Gibson shared that phrase with Robert Downey Jr. during his early addiction recovery and return to cinema. Robert Downey Jr. shared it with the world during an awards ceremony in 2011 with Mel Gibson. His speech chokes me up every single time: https://youtu.be/_AAJuynxnTQ

Life is life. It will always have its ups and downs, challenges, and triumphs. Life wins when I lose my temper or pout and give someone the cold shoulder. When I've given up my power to respond with love and tolerance, I let life kick me around.

To maintain an attitude of love and tolerance, compassion and forgiveness, and to live life on life's terms, I must stay in gratitude, keep my higher power close, and work my recovery program daily.

# CHAPTER NINETEEN

## One Day At A Time

> *"What we really have is a daily reprieve contingent on the maintenance of our spiritual condition."*
> – Alcoholics Anonymous, page 85

*I* used to think that I could rebound instantly if my day was derailed. Now I know that I need to have a "recover the day" plan in place because life situations are mostly "when," not "if."

A member once shared about learning to start his day over at any time using two small words he spoke as prayers—enough and whatever.

He asked his sponsor for help and suggested he could use the Serenity Prayer. His sponsor told him the prayer was too long. That instead, he could use either *enough* or *whatever*. At the very moment he felt his day was ruined, he could end that day right then with *enough,* as in, "I've had enough!" After taking a few slow, deep breaths, he could begin the day anew with *whatever,* as in "Whatever is Your will," as many times as it took in a single day. Before the lesson, if some small disappointment occurred in his day—maybe his debit card wouldn't work at the grocery store, or he was late to an appointment—then his day was ruined. Can you relate? I can.

I wanted to do that—to recognize when I was about to give up on an entire day at eight in the morning because of the circumstances and instead start over again—right then and there.

It's taken me eighteen years to learn to wake up in gratitude and prayer *before* I get out of bed. After thanking my higher power for my sobriety, I recite the Serenity Prayer. Then I get out of bed. I started doing this regularly in April 2022. Yeah. I'm a slower learner than some.

When that pandemic started, I didn't take it seriously. I thought, "Why did this happen to me?" Me.

Sixteen years sober, working a program, and I was still focused on me first. The day that Disneyland closed made the pandemic real for me because I loved visiting Disneyland; I spent most of my free time there, it was my happy place, and to be denied my safe form of escapism hit close to home. I'm sure something different made it real for you. But still, I didn't believe the closure would last.

During those first several months of the pandemic I was faced with how I had used Disneyland as yet another way to avoid myself and my feelings, and I actually worked all the steps on my relationship with Disneyland.

After the meeting locations closed, panic began to rise inside me. I needed to see my tribe weekly, especially now. I went from three meetings a week pre-pandemic to about eleven meetings a week at the beginning of the pandemic. Addicts often overdo things.

I was scared, and I was isolated. I called my sponsor to talk about feeling adrift and needing some structure and discipline. She shared that she had created a checklist—her *protocol*—of daily tasks to keep her moving forward and avoid becoming paralyzed. I'm a list girl and liked the idea. I could envision it supporting me so the panic and anxiety I felt wouldn't shut my thought processes down. I wrote down a list of all the things I could be doing instead of streaming movies and checking the worldwide map of COVID-19 cases and deaths hourly.

I encountered a small setback with that list, however. The way my mind processes information, I somehow interpreted having a list as also having to complete that *entire* list. Every day. All of it. I experienced a few days of overload before I realized what I was doing—my days got worse because I couldn't complete the twenty-five or thirty tasks I'd listed. It was intended to be a suggestion list, but my mind made it a *have-to* list.

I needed something different, more structured to keep me focused, a journal or planner of some sort. After searching the internet extensively, I could not find a single journal or planner for addiction recovery maintenance.

So, I developed my own addiction recovery journal. I knew I needed to practice my recovery program every day. Daily physical exercise was a must. I wanted to feel useful and have direction, so I also set a small goal to work towards. I created the recovery planner for myself to help me remember the basics of my recovery program when I started spinning out of control mentally. I found a way to keep my sanity as the year 2020 progressed.

Creating the *Keep It Simple Habit Tracker*—a recovery journal—kept my mind occupied. I was staying in the present because of that project, and my recovery program was thriving like never before. At the end of the year, when people were lamenting about the past ten months—the dumpster fire of 2020 became a popular reference—I was reflecting instead on the many opportunities for growth that I embraced, which accelerated my recovery at a rate that I still find miraculous. Laser focus would be an accurate choice of words.

I continue to use this habit tracker journal to keep me focused on today while planning out tomorrow, to keep the first things first, and to stay close to my higher power.

The most important part of the habit tracker journal is my morning routine. How I begin the day sets the tone for the rest of the day and helps me to stay present. As a person who works better with a structured day that allows for flexibility, this works for me. I can revisit my morning routine at any given time, even when a day throws me a curveball, like ants invading the kitchen or the cat barfing up her breakfast before I'm fully awake, that kind of thing.

Your morning will most likely look different; this is what mine looks like:

- ✓ Wake up
- ✓ Toilet, teeth, hair
- ✓ Put on clothes
- ✓ Make the bed
- ✓ Drink 16 ounces of water
- ✓ Daily reflection readings
- ✓ Yoga 15-30 minutes
- ✓ Meditation 15-20 minutes
- ✓ Gratitude list

Most days, I write in a journal about what's going on with me—what I'm thinking or feeling or how I walked through a recent situation. Occasionally I'm stumped about what to write. A friend suggested I start with this sentence, "I feel like _____ because _____," and go from there. I rarely go back and read all I've written. Journaling helps me sort out my thoughts in the moment and determine which direction to head next. Sometimes, in the middle of the night,

I wake up with multiple thoughts running through my head. I cannot solve most of the issues at that moment, at three in the morning. I can get up, pull out the journal and write down all those thoughts. When I get them out of my head and onto paper, a stillness returns. Now I can look at those things I wrote later in the day, and I'm free to return to a peaceful slumber.

During the day, I need to maintain contact with others instead of isolating myself, which I do really well. *Isolating, not contact.* I make connections through text messages or phone calls, reaching out to other people, starting the conversation with "How are you?"

I also practice mindfulness several times a day, paying attention to any physical discomfort that may indicate an underlying feeling of restlessness, irritability, or discontent. If I am irritable or discontent, I've learned to practice backtracking by going back to when that feeling began. Sometimes I find that it began days before I really felt it, usually as a result of some incident I didn't honestly address and resolve, like keeping quiet instead of speaking up or saying yes when I meant no.

Some evenings I attend a meeting, either online or in person. Other times I might meet up with friends for dinner before a meeting and catch up.

In the evening, I review my day and complete a checklist of the behaviors I'm working to recognize and change, as suggested by Step Eleven in the book *Alcoholics Anonymous*. I list my wins for the day and review appointments or commitments I've scheduled for the following day. Finally, I get ready for bed. After the lights are out, I thank my higher power for another day of sobriety.

If you'd like to practice a morning routine and journal about your feelings and your progress, all you need is a spiral notebook and a pen or pencil.

All I'm saying here is that I live life one day at a time. I plan for the future and do my best to live in the moment. I love this quote from the Nar-Anon book *Sharing Experience, Strength and Hope* about the past: "I may glance back at the past, but I will not stare." The gifts I've received—tangible and intangible—are beyond anything I could have hoped to receive, allowing me to look forward to my future.

# CHAPTER TWENTY

# The Gifts of Addiction Recovery

As you wrap up this book, you might expect to hear all the wonderful things you will receive if you embark on an addiction recovery program. But the truth is that the gifts you receive by recovering from addiction will look different than what I've received because your needs are different. I can tell you what I've received, and maybe you'll get something that looks similar, but the truth is that while we travel this road together, we drive in different lanes. Sometimes we meet at crossroads and share the same path, then you or I find an offramp that appeals to each of us, and we part ways turning off in a new direction, maybe meeting up again in the future.

The blessings in my life are countless. The gifts I have received from working a recovery program have evolved over time. My relationships are cleaner, clearer, truer. My life is simpler, less complicated, runs more smoothly. Life still presents challenges, but today I know how to face life's challenges and walk through them clean and sober. I can't teach someone how to stay sober. I can only tell you what this journey has been like for me. I hope that my current life in recovery is attractive enough to you that you want what I have and that you decide to choose freedom over slavery using a recovery program and find a community of others.

Today is the first day of the rest of your life. You can choose to do something different, or you can continue along on the path you are on now. It's up to you.

I'll share one more story. When I entered recovery, I did not own one piece of new furniture I had purchased. Everything I owned was second-hand, given to me by someone else. Maybe that sounds amazing to you, that I never had to spend money on my belongings. Except that nothing I had reflected who I was. Well, that's not actually true, is it? Everything I possessed until I got sober reflected exactly who I was—someone who settled for a second-hand life.

I was sober when I purchased my first piece of new furniture. My second husband and I purchased a three-piece living room set—a brand-new hide-a-bed sofa, a love seat, and a chair, all upholstered in beige microfiber. I was around forty years old when I bought my first real adult furniture. Okay, I'll admit, I purchased a couple of Ikea bookcases to hold my Stephen King collection, but other than that, nothing new in the realm of furniture.

Every single piece of furniture I owned—every lamp, every wall hanging, kitchen utensils, computer desk, beds, bed frames, dining room set, all of it—was given to me, to us, by others.

It's all about priorities, and for twenty-plus years mine was marijuana.

At nine years sober, we purchased our second new piece of furniture, a brand-new California King bed. No one ever slept on that bed before us. The last new mattress I owned was the one my parents bought me for my fourteenth birthday, so it had been a while.

Socrates once said, "To know thyself is the beginning of wisdom." One of the biggest gifts I received in recovery is embodying the phrase "know thyself" by learning who I am, my likes and my dislikes, and what I'll stand for and what I won't. My home, my clothes, my friends, and my life all reflect my personality now. And I get to change that whenever I discover something new about myself.

I didn't know that I didn't know who I was until I stopped smoking weed. My greatest achievement as a marijuana addict was how well I rolled joints. My pride as a sober woman in recovery is that I choose who I vote for instead of copying others. I don't have a favorite color; I love all the colors. I prefer jeans and t-shirts over dresses. I like cats more than dogs. I enjoy learning new things. I still like brain puzzles and creating art, cooking, and gardening. I am still stubborn when it comes to some things.

The friends I have today like me for who I am, not because of what I can do for them. I attract healthy, honest, loving people today. We don't always agree with each other, but we do respect each other's differences.

My family members love and respect me, come to me for help, and support me in my struggles and my triumphs.

My life is a result of not just getting sober but staying sober, one day at a time, by working a program of recovery, rebuilding who I could have been before I got all messed up, and evolving from there into the best freaking version of myself so far, every day!

That's it. I've shared my stuff. Today, four months after I started putting all this down on paper, I'm done.

I don't know if you are a marijuana addict. Only you get to decide.

After reading this, if you've decided that you are *not* a marijuana addict, I hope you pass this book along—maybe you could leave it on a bus bench, in a doctor's office, or in a gas station bathroom for the person who needs to hear this.

If you've decided that you may have a problem with marijuana, then I hope this book has offered you some insight, strength, and hope, as well as some tools and resources to help you on your journey. Check out the appendices for additional resources.

Thank you for sticking with me to the end of this particular journey. You must matter to yourself more than you thought to reach the end of this book. Appreciate that about yourself.

You don't have to use marijuana again if you don't want to. Just don't pick up again, no matter what. Get clean and sober for you and no one else, go to meetings, find a sponsor and a higher power that works for you, work the steps, participate in your recovery, give back, and pay it forward. Remember, it's simple, but it's not easy. If it was easy, everyone who thought they might have a problem with a substance would look at it and start their addiction recovery journey.

You've got this. I already know you're an amazing human being. It's time for you to discover that for yourself now.

# RECOVERY RESOURCES

## Substance Abuse Recovery Groups

Many resources are available for those with substance abuse issues as well as for their family and friends.

*For the alcoholic:*
Alcoholics Anonymous – www.alcoholics-anonymous.org

*For the marijuana addict:*
Marijuana Anonymous – www.marijuana-anonymous.org

*For the addict of other substances:*
Narcotics Anonymous – www.na.org

There are also anonymous support groups that meet for cocaine, prescription pills, overeating or eating disorders, sex and love, co-dependency and others. Search the substance or issue followed by the word "anonymous" to get started.

## Support for Families & Friends of Addicts and/or Alcoholics

*For the loved ones of alcoholics:*
Al-Anon Family Groups – www.al-anon.org

*For the loved ones of marijuana addicts:*
Mar-Anon Family Groups – www.mar-anon.org

*For the loved ones of addicts:*
Nar-Anon Family Groups – www.nar-anon.org

# A Few Recovery Prayers and Slogans

### Serenity Prayer
*God, grant me the Serenity
to Accept the things I cannot change,
Courage to change the things I can,
and the Wisdom to know the difference.*

### Third Step Prayer from *Life With Hope*
*Higher Power,
I have tried to control the uncontrollable for far too long,
I ask that you take this burden from me.
I acknowledge that my life has become unmanageable,
I ask for your care and guidance.
Grant me honesty, courage, humility and strength
to face that which keeps me from you and others.
I give this life to you to do with as you will.*

### Set Aside Prayer
*Lord, today help me set aside
Everything I think I know about You,
Everything I think I know about myself,
Everything I think I know about others, and
Everything I think I know about my own recovery
for a new experience in myself,
a new experience in my fellows,
and my own recovery.*

## Common Recovery Slogans

Easy Does It

Keep It Simple

One Day At A Time

Let Go and Let God

Principles Before Personalities

Progress Not Perfection

Hug the Cactus

Live and Let Live

# Recommended Reading in Recovery

I've read each of these titles and feel they are of benefit to anyone traveling on this journey of living.

**Twelve Step Recovery literature – Basic Texts**
*Alcoholics Anonymous* by A.A. World Services
*It Works: How and Why* by Narcotics Anonymous
*Life with Hope* by Marijuana Anonymous
*Narcotics Anonymous* by Narcotics Anonymous
*Twelve Steps and Twelve Traditions* by A.A. World Services

**Other recovery literature based on the Twelve Steps and Twelve Traditions**
*Drop The Rock: Removing Character Defects – Steps 6 and 7* by Todd W., Sara S.
*Drop the Rock: The Ripple Effect – Using Step 10 to work Steps 6 & 7 Everyday* by Fred H.
*Experience, Strength, and Hope* by A.A. World Services, Inc.
*Living Sober* by A.A. World Services, Inc.
*A New Pair of Glasses* by Chuck C.
*The Twelve Steps for Everyone: Who Wants Them* by Jerry Hirschfield, Ph.D.

**Literature written in support of recovery**
*Idiot* by Laura Clery
*Miracle Morning for Addiction Recovery* by Hal Elrod, Joe Polish and Anna David

**Powerful Personal Development literature**
*The Alchemist* by Paulo Coelho
*Awareness: Conversations with the Masters* by Anthony de Mello
*Be Here Now* by Ram Dass
*Bird by Bird: Some Instructions on Writing and Life* by Anne Lamott

*Braving The Wilderness* by Brené Brown, Ph.D.
*Change Your Brain, Change Your Life* by Dr. Daniel Amen
*Daring Greatly* by Brené Brown, PhD
*Emotional Intelligence: Why It Can Matter More Than IQ* by Daniel Goleman
*The Four Agreements: A Practical Guide to Personal Freedom* by Don Miguel Ruiz
*Get Off Your "BUT": How to End Self Sabotage and Stand Up for Yourself* by Sean Stephenson
*Homecoming: Reclaiming and Championing Your Inner Child* by John Bradshaw
*How Can I Help? Stories and Reflections of Service* by Ram Dass, Paul Gorman
*How To Be Here* by Rob Bell
*Illusions: The Adventures of a Reluctant Messiah* by Richard Bach
*The Last Letter: Embracing Pain to Create a Meaningful Life* by Andy Chaleff
*Life's Golden Ticket: A Story About Second Chances* by Brendon Burchard
*Man's Search For Meaning* by Viktor Frankl
*Mindset: The New Psychology* of Success by Carol Dweck, Ph.D.
*The Most Magnificent Thing* by Asley Spires
*My Stroke of Insight: A Brain Scientist's Personal Journey* by Jill Bolte Taylor
*The Noticer: Sometimes, all a person needs is a little perspective* by Andy Andrews
*The Race: Life's Greatest Lesson* by Dee Groberg
*Traveling Mercies: Some Thoughts on Faith* by Anne Lamott
*The Untethered Soul: The Journey Beyond Yourself* by Michael A. Singer
*The Velveteen Rabbit* by Margery Williams
*Way of the Peaceful Warrior: A Book that Changes Lives* by Dan Millman

*When Things Fall Apart: Heart Advice for Difficult Times* by Pema Chodron

*The Wounded Healer: A Journey in Radical Self-Love* by Andy Chaleff

# ACKNOWLEDGMENTS

*This is the space where I thank everyone who helped me along the way.*

*My parents for bringing me into the world.*

*To them, and every other person who served as, and will serve as, my teacher in this journey called life.*

*My editor, who made this book something more.*

*Thanks to the Universe, to my Creator, for giving me an opportunity to serve.*

# AUTHOR BIO

Kathy D. was born in Los Angeles and grew up in Orange County, California. Her arrest in 2003 for felony marijuana cultivation was the beginning of the end of her twenty-plus years of alcoholism and drug addiction. First reluctant, she chose sobriety, and eventually embraced a program of recovery. Now she carries the message of recovery and helps others to find freedom in sobriety. Kathy enjoys expanding her knowledge about the human condition, and enjoys cooking, gardening, and creating original arts and crafts. She loves Disneyland.

*Kathy has four children and seven grandchildren. She and her husband, Ron, live in Palm Desert, California with their cat, Jingles.*

Love this book? I'd be grateful if you'd leave a review! Every review is important, and it matters a *lot!*

Please, head over to wherever you purchased this book to leave an honest review for me. Thank you.

Made in the USA
Monee, IL
27 March 2023